KU-594-354

Brussels

Front cover and below: aspects of the Grand-Place

The Cathédrale des Sts-Michel-et-Gudule • Beautiful stained glass windows in the choir depict Louis II and his wife *(page 37)*

Atomium • A symbol of the city, this metallic 1950s sculpture rises above the toy-town buildings of Mini-Europe *(page 54)*

Manneken-Pis •
The city's famously cheeky statue
(page 35)

Parc du Cinquantenaire •
It features a monumental arch and three museums *(page 48)*

The Grand-Place This focal point of the city's daily life is simply one of the loveliest squares in the world *(page 28)*

Antwerp's Grote Markt A 16th-century square with a fountain of the heroic Silvius Brabo at its centre *(page 62)*

Ghent The city has numerous attractions, including the picturesque Korenlei *(page 82)*

Place Royale It lies at the heart of Royal Brussels, with the church of St-Jacques-sur-Coudenberg *(page 40)*

Bruges The 13th-century Belfry towers over its main square, the Markt *(page 70)*

The Old England Department Store One of many lovely Art Nouveau buildings, it now houses a music museum *(page 41)*

CONTENTS

92

8

52

50

89

34

INTRODUCTION

Brussels is the capital of Belgium, a small Western European country of 10 million people set between the Netherlands in the north, France in the south and Germany in the east. When Belgium gained its independence in 1830, Brussels was at first cast in a purely domestic role. Since the end of World War II, however, this city of one million has evolved into an international centre. The headquarters of NATO are here, and the city hosts several key institutions of the European Union (EU), an organisation that has transformed the political and economic climate of the continent. Although Strasbourg and Luxembourg also host EU institutions, no one denies that Brussels is the focal point and heartbeat of the Union. Brussels is an international and cosmopolitan city, where many people speak at least two languages, and English speakers have few problems being understood, where the demand for office space is sky-high, and the international airport is one of the fastest-growing in Europe.

Historic Town

One might imagine a 21st-century metropolis of high-rise blocks, with clogged motorways and streets that empty after 5pm. But nothing could be further from the truth. The city's history is a long and rich tapestry dating back many centuries before Belgian independence.

Small by international standards – the city centre can be crossed on foot in about 30 minutes – it is people-friendly. It has a buoyant native population that fills the streets with vibrancy by day and makes it one of the safest of the world's major cities by night. It is a city of delights, and one

The Town Hall on the Grand-Place

that has the capability to constantly surprise with its architecture, gastronomy and nightlife.

Brussels has been at the heart of European history for much of the last millennium. A trading town on the lucrative route from Eastern Europe to England, it was the leading northern city of the vast Spanish European Empire during the 17th century and, after Vienna, of the wealthy Habsburg Austro-Hungarian Empire in the 18th century. However, though Brussels continues to flirt with Europe, it has not yet forgotten that it is first and foremost a Belgian city.

Trading Places

In addition to being a diplomatic centre, it has always been a working and trading town. The pearl that is the old heart of Brussels began its life around the seed of a marketplace in the 14th century. You will discover that many of the street names in the old town hark back to this time, when traders would set up stalls along the narrow, cobbled alleys. Cheese Market, Chicken Market, Grass Market and Butchers' Row – the names conjure up images of bustling medieval Brussels. These same streets still earn their keep, sustaining modern

European institutions

visitors with bars and restaurants. The guilds that controlled the skilled trades built large and ornate houses in the centre of town as a visual affirmation of their wealth and influence. They extended a largely benevolent but, when required, brutal control over Brussels' artisans, who were admired around Europe for their skill and workmanship. On

Théâtre Royal de la Monnaie

Coudenberg, a hill east of the old town, sat royal and ducal palaces and buildings to house visiting foreign emissaries sent to negotiate with the occupants of the neighbouring palaces.

A dazzling 17th-century town square, the Grand-Place, takes one's breath away with its ornate stonework and gilt decoration. The 14th-century Town Hall is one of the most beautiful examples of civic architecture in Europe. And the narrow streets that surround it are replete with original architectural detail. The skyline on the hill above was transformed during the 18th century in the Louis XVI style, which was *de rigueur* at the time. The palace is still in use by today's Belgian royal family, but it now sits side-by-side with museums dedicated to the arts, filled with collections encompassing the finest Belgian artists and canvasses by a wealth of European masters. In the 19th century, King Leopold II gave life to a number of civil construction projects; and in the 20th century, Brussels continued to make architectural history

On parade

with the futuristic Atomium (completed in 1958, just in time for Brussels to host the World's Fair). Almost every corner of the city offers an architectural treat: from Romanesque churches to Gothic towers and Baroque theatres, and a wealth of Art Nouveau – in fact no architecture buff should leave Brussels dissatisfied.

Natives and Foreigners

Thanks to the presence of the EU and NATO, it is said that there are more decision-makers here than in any other city on earth. And yet, when you walk the streets, Brussels does not feel like a powerhouse. It has the gentility and civility of a dowager duchess and it never seems to throw its considerable weight around. Perhaps this is because, even today, the city is not only concerned about world affairs. For every foreign diplomat, there is a shopkeeper, and this 'real activity' helps the city to maintain its pragmatic air.

There is relatively little friction between the natives and the 'army' of foreigners who make Brussels their temporary home. But then this isn't the first foreign 'invasion' to confront the city. The character of the city and its people has been shaped by their country's geography, sandwiched as it has been between two seemingly constantly warring dynasties. Numerous decisive battles have taken place on Belgian soil, Waterloo being but one. Foreigners have usurped this land on many occasions, including both world wars. Today's bloodless diplomatic 'coups' are designed to consign all of this to history.

In the midst of European détente, Belgium's internal strife may astonish visitors, but with several disparate groups making up the population, differences of opinion on language, education and social services are still being fought out in council chambers and the press. The Flemish north of the country is Dutch-speaking and the Walloon south is French-speaking. There is also a small German-speaking enclave in the east. Brussels caters to both major languages, but beyond the capital multilingual signs are less evident.

Despite this domestic friction, the Belgians have a philosophical attitude to life. There's a great deal to like about people who decorate their metro stations with canvasses by their best known contemporary artists, and the sides of houses with cartoon or comic-strip images. Their natural love of imagery makes Brussels rich in cinema, photography, sculpture and art. With national ballet, opera and theatre companies, there is no shortage of high art, but in addition Brussels embraces with ease novel genres and groundbreaking work.

Underground Art

The Brussels metro provides transport – and more. Art has gone underground, transforming commuter platforms with a wealth of colour and style. All the works on display are by famous Belgian artists. The Bourse station features a revolving ceiling sculpture by Pol Bury (1922–2005) and a dream-like painting of tram passengers by the great Surrealist Paul Delvaux (1897–1994). At Comte de Flandre station, 16 soaring bronze figures by Paul van Hoeydonck (b.1925), titled *16 x Icarus*, invade the tunnel. The characters of Belgium's comic-strip *Tintin* are to be found covering the walls of Stockel station.

The city's public transport company, STIB, publishes a brochure describing the art on display in the metro, with several suggested itineraries to follow.

When Belgians do things, they do them with a passion. Where else would you be able to choose from around 500 different domestic beers, or eat mussels cooked in 20 different styles? The many restaurants and bars in the city pay testament to Brussels' love of the good life, and you should take advantage of many opportunities to join the informal party.

Royal collector

King Leopold II caught the 19th-century collecting 'bug'. He used money from his personal fortune to construct the vast and varied collection of the Royal Museum of Central Africa. Leopold personally supervised the design of the building that houses it.

This passion has also extended to collecting, with a multitude of museums for visitors to explore. Although many attractions are found in the compact city centre, many others are located within the 19 *communes* or separate small towns that make up the Brussels-Capital Region. These are only a short tram ride away, or one or two stops on the metro. Each commune has a particular character – from tree-lined bourgeois districts to gritty working-class neighbourhoods. As Europe has extended a helping hand to refugees from many countries, some areas now have burgeoning African, Asian and Arab populations. Exploring at least one of these *communes* allows you to discover more of the real Brussels; for underneath its charms – the majestic old buildings, impressive museum collections and pretty streets – the city has a complex and alluring personality.

Brussels is full of surprises. City dwellers have vast swathes of forest to enjoy, just a tram ride from the city centre. To those who expect bland Euroland, Brussels presents a historical time capsule. And to those who imagine a living museum, they discover a 21st-century society thoroughly in tune with the 'now'. Allow yourself to enjoy all this about Brussels; it's rare to find a place where this combination works so well.

A BRIEF HISTORY

In 57BC, Julius Caesar came to Belgium and, after a great deal of trouble with a population he described as 'the bravest of all the peoples of Gaul', conquered the country. At that time, Brussels did not yet exist as a city, although two Roman roads had been built through its present site (one of which is still called chaussée Romaine). From the evidence of the bronzes, coins and funeral urns found, a number of dignitaries and officers had villas constructed in the area some decades later. During the 450 years of Roman rule, the Belgae of the southern region became heavily Latinised, while the north was left in the end to Germanic tribes.

Brussels first appeared on the scene around AD600 when St Géry, the Bishop of Cambrai, is said to have built a church at the small settlement here. At this time and later, it was known variously as Brosella, Brucella, Bruocsella, Bruohsella, Bruesella and Borsella, with as many different meanings suggested by historians. Selections include 'stork's nest' and 'dwelling near the bridge', but the most generally accepted seems to be 'dwelling in the marshes'. This supposedly refers to three swampy islands in the now paved-over River Senne, on which the first castle and church were built.

Local hero: crusader Godfrey of Bouillon, on place Royale

The Middle Ages

The foundation of the city proper dates back officially to AD979, when a fortress was erected here by Charles,

Duke of Lower Lorraine, the brother of Carolingian King Lothair of France. In the following century, the town began to take shape when, in 1047, Count Lambert II of Louvain built a new castle on the Coudenberg Heights (today called place Royale), surrounded by a group of houses within a walled compound. The lack of space inside meant that less-fortunate artisans and peasants were left unprotected outside the ramparts, thus laying the foundations for the long struggle between the city's haves and have-nots.

In the 12th century, Brussels rose to prominence in the province of Brabant, gaining in prosperity due to its role as a centre of gold and silversmithing and as a station on the commercial route between the trading centres of Cologne and Bruges. By 1235 the city's administration was in the hands of an oligarchy of seven patrician families known as *lignages*. Each contributed an *échevin*, or alderman, to serve

The River Senne

Most major cities have a body of water nearby. They may be seaports, or set on river mouths, or at crossing points on rivers inland. But Brussels does not have a river. Or does it?

Well, in fact, it does. The city was originally founded on the River Senne, whose path cut directly through the centre of the old town. However, when the river became dirty and polluted following the Industrial Revolution, the people of Brussels decided on a novel and innovative solution; they would simply put the river out of sight. Work began in 1867 and was allied with a comprehensive plan by Mayor Jules Anspach to create a number of fine boulevards in the newly created landscape above. A series of culverts confined the waters and a network of sewers drained effluent from all parts of the city. Finally, the river disappeared under brick arcades, although it still flows to the present day.

on the council. Brussels expanded its trade in precious metals with international orders for minting coins. It also started a prosperous textile industry using wool imported from England. However, with male workers demanding higher wages and better working conditions, the lords began to look elsewhere for labour, and a number of *béguinages* (communities of religious lay women) were established, partly as a source of cheap and docile workers.

Porte de Hal, the city's only surviving medieval gate

The Brussels bourgeoisie was already growing prosperous and willful. In 1291 Duke Jean I had to make tax and toll concessions to their municipal treasury. In an attempt to forestall the problems of dealing with recalcitrant artisans, the ruling oligarchy claimed the right of approval over the formation of the craft guilds – a restriction that strongly riled the artisans.

The Brussels craftsmen staged a revolt demanding a greater say in city government. Some 36 professional groups were each allowed to send representatives to administer the town's affairs. However, Brussels' first attempt at democracy came to an abrupt end just three years later, when the army of Duke Jean II and the patrician cavalry of the *lignages* defeated the artisans in the bloody battle of Vilvoorde (1306). For the next 50 years the artisans were forbidden to bear arms, and uprisings rumbled on until guild privileges were gradually reinstated for certain professions.

The Burgundians

At the end of the 14th century the dukes of Burgundy took control of Brussels from their seat in Bruges, and under them good times were to be had. However, the demand for Brussels cloth declined, as at the same time textiles manufactured in England became more competitive. By 1430 Brussels cloth had practically disappeared from international markets. With no work, many artisans were forced to leave the city, and the population declined. Brussels compensated for the collapse of the textile industry by turning to tapestry weaving, for which it became renowned. The demand for skilled Brussels weavers became intense. With demand rising for other skills as well, the craft guilds began to reform and gain strength.

The painter Jan van Eyck is remembered in Bruges

The Burgundian era was a golden age for the arts. Jan van Eyck, Rogier van der Weyden, Hans Memling and Dirk Bouts were only the best known of a superb group of 15th-century Flemish painters. Civic pride was reflected in the great Gothic town halls that sprang up all across Belgium, though none ever surpassed Brussels' own great jewel in the Grand-Place, surrounded by equally grand guild houses.

The dukes – Philip the Bold, John the Fearless and Philip the Good – asserted their supremacy with pageants and festivities to keep the people happy. However, their dominance began to disintegrate in wars with Louis XI of France, and before long the city was beset with revolts, famine and plague. Charles the Bold, Philip the Good's successor, was in turn succeeded by his daughter Mary, who married Maximilian of Austria and thus brought the Habsburgs to Brussels.

Charles the Bold

Habsburg Rule

In 1515 Maximilian's grandson, the future Charles V, made his *Joyeuse Entrée* into Brussels as its new archduke. He moved into the palace on the Coudenberg, which was to be his only fixed residence during his peripatetic reign as king of Spain and Holy Roman Emperor. As Bruges lost its influence, Brussels became the capital of the Low Countries (roughly following the borders of what is now Belgium and Holland), as well as a great European centre of trade and culture.

The renowned Dutch philosopher Erasmus also enjoyed the city's pleasant atmosphere, and Pieter Bruegel the Elder came to Brussels to paint his marvellous studies of life in the Low Countries. Brussels' thriving trade in luxury goods at this time was enhanced by the vogue of its lace-makers and the expertise of its highly prized gunsmiths.

The *Ommegang*, or 'walk-around', the most spectacular of Brussels' festivities, gave the resident Renaissance nobility and gentry a chance to show off their riches in a procession around the city. Originally a religious celebration of a miraculous statue of the Virgin (brought to the city in 1348), it soon became an undisguised assertion of the nobility's civic authority. The *Ommegang* is still held every year in early July in the Grand-Place. It was at the event, in 1549, when Charles V introduced his son from Spain to the citizens of Brussels; in 1555, Charles abdicated in his son's favour. The Belgians viewed the new King Philip II with suspicion.

Inquisitions, Shells and Beheadings

During Charles' reign, Calvinists had arrived in Brussels, and the people of the Low Countries embraced the Reformation with enthusiasm. Soon, the spiritual rebellion against Catholicism became identified with the nationalist rebellion against Spanish rule, and discontent grew. Charles only dimly perceived the seriousness of this threat to Spanish power and was lax in enforcing his powers. However, Philip, who disliked his northern subjects, was less easygoing. He brought in the inquisitors and surrounded himself with Spanish soldiers, and blood began to flow.

Nationalist resistance was led by William of Nassau, Prince of Orange. Philip, who in 1559 headed back to Spain, sent the Duke of Alba – the 'bloody duke' – to quash the revolt. Two leading landowners, counts Egmont and Hornes, more nationalists than rebels, were executed in the Grand-Place in 1568. However, the Prince of Orange was able to drive out the Spanish in 1576, whereupon Brussels enacted ferocious anti-Catholic legislation. In 1581 the Catholic religion was simply 'abolished'.

Count Egmont

Count Egmont is remembered not just through the famous statue of him and Hornes on place du Petit-Sablon, but also through a play written by Goethe and an overture, *Egmont*, by Beethoven (opus 84).

This outraged Philip, who sent a large army, under the command of Alexander Farnese, to re-occupy the city. The southern provinces of the Low Countries returned to Spain and Catholicism, but the northern provinces (now the Netherlands) succeeded in breaking away and remained largely Protestant. Brussels saw a flood of Jesuits, monks and nuns to reinforce the Catholic Counter-Reformation.

Under the rule of Philip's daughter, Archduchess Isabella, and her husband, Archduke Albert of Austria, Brussels returned to a general semblance of order (1599–1633). Life in the

Statue of counts Egmont and Hornes in place du Petit-Sablon

capital became quite fashionable, with a constant flow of ambassadors, generals, bishops and cardinals bringing a new cosmopolitan air to the court of the governors-general around the Sablon quarter. The spirit of the age found great artistic expression in the sumptuous contours of Flemish Baroque, which reached its peak with the magnificent paintings of Peter Paul Rubens.

At this time, Brussels was a haven for political exiles – Marie de Medici, Christina of Sweden, the dukes of Bouillon and Vendôme and the sons of Charles I of England. However, by the end of the century it was not quite so safe. In 1695 Louis XIV of France took his revenge for the Dutch and English shelling of his coastal towns with the wanton bombardment of Brussels. Marshal de Villeroy's army of 70,000 men occupied Anderlecht and set up its cannons at the gate of Ninove. For two days, shells and cannonballs fell on some 4,000 buildings, killing 1,000 people, yet the city did not surrender. The Grand-Place was badly damaged, yet the Town Hall's superb belltower survived.

Revolution to Revolution

In 1701 a dynastic wrangle brought war in Europe, and in the peace that followed, control of the southern Low Countries passed to the Austrian Habsburgs. The subsequent period of growth in Belgium was subsidised by trade links controlled by Vienna. Emperor Joseph II ruled Belgium in the last part of the 18th century with a form of enlightened despotism. His religious reforms and judicial liberalisation upset the conservative Belgians, and the centralised Vienna-controlled administration jarred with its habit of local autonomy, and nowhere more so than in Brussels.

This was at a time when the Americans had thrown off the British yoke, and the French were getting rid of their royal one. In January 1790 the old patrician families of Brussels staged a revolt, which drove the Austrians out and restored their ancient privileges under the 'Etats Belges Unis' (United Belgian States). The revolutionary regime was short-lived: in December, the Austrians returned, only to be ousted in 1792 by the French Revolutionary army. In 1793 the French decided simply to annex Belgium. Their influence was mixed. Increased trade with France brought more affluence, but museums and libraries were pillaged, and many able-bodied men were press-ganged into the Revolutionary army.

In the winter of 1813–14, Brussels saw the French troops depart, only for them to be replaced by Russians, Prussians, Dutch and, finally, by the British, waiting for orders to go into battle with Napoleon in 1815. The rendezvous was around 20km (12 miles) away, at Waterloo, on 18 June.

Napoleon's defeat and the resulting Congress of Vienna brought 16 years of Dutch rule to Belgium, resurrecting old tensions and creating new ones. During Napoleon's rule, the national language was French. Even in Flanders, French was the language of the nobility and bourgeoisie. King William of Orange introduced Dutch, previously spoken only by the lower ranks of society, into schools, municipal government and courts. French-speaking teachers were upset by the imposition of Dutch and taught the sciences in Latin. Catholics were upset by the removal of schools from church control, and liberals were upset by press censorship.

Colonne du Congrès, commemorating independence

Independence at Last

With Paris overthrowing its monarch in July 1830, revolt was in the air. In August liberal journalists were active in Brussels, and workers were demonstrating against low pay and poor living conditions. At a performance of Daniel Auber's opera *La Muette de Portici* on 25 August, the rousing aria *Amour Sacré de la Patrie* (Sacred Love of the Fatherland) raised the blood of the bourgeois audience. Belgians of all classes came out on to the streets in a series of civil disturbances. Rioters attacked the Palais de Justice, and sacked the homes of government ministers, while the police and army stood by. In September, King William sent troops to Brussels, and there were many casualties on both sides; when Belgium's independence was recognised on 21 July 1831, the keys of the capital were handed over to the country's new king, Leopold of Saxe-Coburg.

With independence came high economic growth but also social, political and religious conflicts. Tensions were high between Catholics and liberals, and between Flemings (Dutch-speaking Belgians in the north) and Walloons (French-speaking Belgians in the south). Conservative Catholic provinces resisted universal suffrage and so maintained control over the government. This fuelled their fight with the liberals of the capital over education and church power. Although Brussels was nominally bilingual, French was increasingly dominant in business and state administration. The Flemings campaigned with increasing indignation for greater use of their language in the universities and law courts.

Throughout the 19th century and particularly during the reign of Leopold II (1865–1909), industrial expansion and imperial adventures in Africa, particularly in the Congo, brought great prosperity to Brussels. There was a flurry of construction, with mansions and commercial buildings rising up along the wide avenues and boulevards. As ever, the products of the luxury industries – textiles, furniture, lace, fine porcelain, paper and books – were at a premium.

Leopold II

Brussels was once again a refuge for political exiles, notably from Poland, Italy, France and Russia. Germany's Friedrich Engels and Karl Marx organised the socialist German Workers' Club at Le Cygne on the Grand-Place. The two wrote the *Communist Manifesto* here, and then were kicked out of Belgium in 1848, when it was feared that their writings and ideas might reproduce the latest Paris Revolution. There was also an explosion of artistic achievement in the capital. Painters including James Ensor, Félicien Rops and Fernand Khnopff came together in the Groupe des XX in 1883.

Art Nouveau staircase in the Musée Horta (see page 51)

Brussels was also a major centre of Art Nouveau architecture under the leadership of both Victor Horta and Paul Hankar.

World Wars and International Leadership

Belgium's historic vulnerability to invasion was displayed again in August 1914, when Kaiser Wilhelm's German armies occupied Brussels. The capital put up a heroic passive resistance, and when the Germans were defeated, Belgium expressed its new-found sense of national unity in the introduction of universal suffrage, the right to strike, a Flemish university and, finally, a truce in the church-school conflict. In the 1930s there was the emergence in Brussels, as in other

European capitals, of new fascist groups drawing on social discontent and primitive chauvinism. The fascist leader Léon Degrelle achieved that which had eluded other Belgian leaders: he united Catholics, liberals and socialists in a combined effort to defeat him, resoundingly, in the 1937 elections. These grim times offered the best breeding ground for a flight into the Surrealist art of René Magritte and Paul Delvaux, and the comic-strip escapism of Hergé's *Tintin*.

Then came World War II and another German occupation. The Nazi invaders found a few fascist collaborators to prepare Belgium for integration into the Reich, and King Leopold III caused controversy with his passive acceptance of the invasion.

After the war Belgium held a referendum in which King Leopold gained a majority of 58 percent. However, not having a majority in each province, he refused to be reinstated and was succeeded in 1951 by his son Baudouin. While Flemings and Walloons continued to squabble, Belgium took on a new role as the internationalist capital of Western Europe and the Atlantic alliance. In 1957 the EEC (now the European Union) established its headquarters in Brussels. The following year the city staged a very successful World's Fair based on the theme of building a better world for mankind, and in 1960 divested itself of its African colonies.

NATO moved its headquarters to Brussels in 1967, and the city subsequently attracted around a quarter of a million permanent foreign residents to work in military organisations and the multinational offices of commerce. In the 1980s and 1990s, while the Belgian government introduced regional government to allow greater local decision-making, Brussels continued in its role as the central lynchpin in Europe. With the EU having expanded up to the borders of the old Soviet Union, the city's role as the focal point for the continent continues to develop.

Historical Landmarks

AD979 Founding of the city with the building of a fortress.

1047 Construction of the first city wall.

1303 Uprising of craftsmen demanding greater say in city government.

1401 Construction of the Town Hall begins.

1406 Dukes of Burgundy take control of Brussels.

1515 The future emperor Charles V becomes Archduke of Brabant.

1531 Brussels becomes the capital of the Spanish Netherlands.

1555 Charles V abdicates. Brussels is subject to Philip II of Spain.

1568 Belgian counts Egmont and Hornes beheaded for high treason.

1576 Under the Prince of Orange, Brussels revolts and drives out the Spanish, but the latter re-occupy the city in 1585.

1599 Archduchess Isabella restores order in the city.

1695 Louis XIV of France bombards Brussels.

1713 Under the Treaty of Utrecht, Brussels becomes subject to Austria.

1789 Brabant Revolution drives out the Austrians, but is crushed the following year by Austria and France.

1794 Belgium is annexed by France.

1815 The French are defeated at Waterloo. Congress of Vienna cedes Belgium to the Netherlands; William of Orange is crowned.

1830 Belgian Revolution begins in Brussels, leading to independence.

1831 Leopold of Saxe-Coburg is made first king of the Belgians.

1914–18 World War I: most of Belgium is occupied by German army.

1940–5 World War II: Belgium is again occupied by Germany.

1951 King Leopold III abdicates in favour of his son, Baudouin.

1957 The EEC (European Union) makes its headquarters in Brussels.

1967 NATO's headquarters are moved to Brussels.

1993 King Baudouin is succeeded by Albert II.

1994 Brussels-Capital becomes one of three federal regions in Belgium.

1995 Brabant province, surrounding Brussels, separates into Dutch-speaking Flemish Brabant and French-speaking Walloon Brabant.

2002 The euro replaces the Belgian franc as the national currency.

2006 The Atomium reopens after a two-year refurbishment.

WHERE TO GO

The city of Brussels is made up of 19 *communes* or boroughs, each with its own council, administration and police force. Every *commune* has a distinctive character based on its history, major industry and social make-up. The central *commune* is the only one called Brussels, but most people travelling to the city know the metropolitan conurbation as a whole by this name.

A well-organised, integrated and inexpensive public transport system makes the greater Brussels area easy to explore. Central Brussels is compact and, with comfortable footwear, is a good destination for walking.

This book divides the city into a number of easy-to-follow sections, taking central Brussels first and then

Two languages

In bilingual Brussels, street and building names appear in both French and Dutch. For simplicity, in this book we have used only the French names (French is spoken by 90 percent of the population as a first or second language). For Flanders, where the Dutch language prevails, we have followed the local practice in citing place names.

exploring the highlights of the surrounding *communes*, as well as the battlefield at Waterloo, 15km (9 miles) from the city. We also include excursions to the cities of Antwerp, Bruges and Ghent.

THE HEART OF THE CITY

In the Middle Ages, Brussels was surrounded by a protective wall, with access through seven gates. Inside the wall is an area of 3km by 2km (2 miles by 1½ miles), a network of narrow cobbled streets, with the Coudenberg hill marking the city's highest point. When Napoleon Bonaparte took control of Brussels in 1799, he decided to tear down the wall and create wide boulevards around the city. These still exist today as the *petite ceinture* or inner ring road, a four- to six-lane highway. It is the *petite ceinture* that, for the most part, creates the boundary between the *commune* of Brussels and the surrounding *communes* of the city.

The Grand-Place

There are some places in the world where no matter how wonderful you hear they are, nothing prepares you for seeing them. The **Grand-Place** is one such place. The beauty is almost overwhelming, the skill of the masons awe-inspiring. Yet the square also has a very human quality, with numerous cafés where you can sit and watch the world go by.

The Maison du Roi fronts one corner of the Grand-Place

The Grand-Place has long been the heart of the city. Its Dutch name, Grote Markt, indicates that it was developed as the main marketplace. This part of town became Brussels' commercial heartland at the end of the first millennium, when nearby marshes were drained, creating land for building.

Markets grew up haphazardly, but towards the end of the 13th century, it was clear that a large open area would have to be planned, and houses were demolished to create the space. The foundation stone of the Hôtel de Ville (Town Hall) was laid in 1401 and soon powerful corporations began building their guild houses close to this symbol of secular power.

These buildings were already 200 years old when the League of Augsburg – an alliance between the United Provinces (Holland), Britain, Spain and Germany – went to war with the French under Louis XIV, the Sun King. In 1695, Louis ordered the bombardment of Brussels. On 13 August, 70,000 men laid siege to the walls, and cannonballs began to rain down, devastating the Grand-Place. Only the spire of the Hôtel de Ville and the façades of three houses remained intact.

In the aftermath of this devastation, the town council decided that a new Grand-Place would be planned and controlled. It approved or vetoed the design of each house fronting the square, resulting in the Grand-Place we see today.

The Hôtel de Ville

The **Hôtel de Ville** (Town Hall; guided tours in English: Apr–Sept Tues and Wed 3.15pm, Sun 10.45am and 12.15pm; Oct–Mar Tues and Wed 3.15pm; admission fee), resplendent following renovation work in the 1990s, is a magnificent building, whose construction sent an important message about the power that ruled Brussels at the time. While other communities were concentrating their efforts on erecting grand religious buildings, the leaders of Brussels chose to celebrate the civic side of life. The design is an amalgam of covered market and

Flowers & festivals

Flowers & festivals

Between March and October, the Grand-Place is the location of a flower market (Tues–Sun). It is also the venue of many Brussels festivals, such as the annual Burgundian Ommegang parade in July, when the city's guilds and corporations come together to celebrate their illustrious histories.

fortified mansion, and each façade was rebuilt to the original plans following the bombardment of 1695. The 96-m (312-ft) tower, dating from the 1450s, replaced an earlier belfry. A statue of the Archangel Michael, the city's patron, tops the tower. A series of first-floor galleries and arcades brings coherence to these two separate elements. The Lion Staircase, which now forms the main entrance, was added later (the lion statues in 1770). The coving around the portal features sculptures of eight prophets, while the friezes between the first and second floors depict leading ducal luminaries.

The interior is equally attractive. The highly decorated meeting hall is still home to the council of the *commune*, while the court room is now used for weddings. One wall of the David and Bathsheba Room is filled with a 1520 tapestry showing Bathsheba at the fountain. Walls in corridors and halls pay tribute in sculpture and paintings to the guildsmen who brought the town prosperity, and the royal families who brought it power. The Tourist Office of Brussels is on the ground floor.

Houses of the Dukes and Guilds

Travelling from the Hôtel de Ville in a clockwise direction around the Grand-Place, the first highlight is No. 7, **Le Renard** (meaning 'the fox', in French), or House of the Haberdashers, built in 1699. The name refers to Marc de Vos (Dutch for fox), one of its architects. It is adorned with statues representing the four continents known at that time, and Justice blindfolded. **Le Cornet**, next door at No. 6, was the boatmen's guild house and has a superb Italianate-Flemish frontage designed by Antoine Pastorana. At No. 5, **La Louve** (1696) is famed for a statue of Romulus and Remus being suckled by a she-wolf *(la louve)*, which gives the house its name. Above this are four statues representing Truth, Falsehood, Peace and Discord. **Le Sac** at No. 4, the House of Coopers and Cabinetmakers, has one of the façades that remained standing after the French bombardment. Much of it dates from the 1640s, although Pastorana added the upper ornamentation. The house takes its name from

Maison du Roi detail

the frieze of a man taking something out of a *sac* (bag), which can be found above the door. No. 3, **La Brouette** (The Wheelbarrow) was House of the Tallow or Grease-Merchants, and is now a café. On the corner is **Le Roy d'Espagne** (King of Spain's House), which belonged to the guild of bakers. Its classical lines have been attributed to the architect and sculptor Jean Cosyn, and the octagonal dome that tops it – crowned with a gilded weathervane symbolising Fame – adds elegance to the square. Le Roy d'Espagne is now a café.

The northern side of the square, opposite the Hôtel de Ville, is dominated by the large and ornate **Maison du Roi** (King's House), built on the site of the Bread Market between 1515 and 1536. The rights to this piece of land passed through the

Beer-making at the Musée de la Brasserie (Brewing Museum)

dukes of Burgundy to Emperor Charles V (who was also King of Spain), hence the house's name. In the 1870s, Mayor Charles Buls wanted to redesign the house. Architect Pierre-Victor Jamaer retained the Gothic style, adding the flamboyant tower and arcades. Although the façade is not to everyone's taste, you should enjoy the **Musée de la Ville de Bruxelles** (Museum of the City of Brussels; open Tues–Sun 10am–5pm; admission fee) inside. Its rooms have exhibits relating to the city's urban development and political and social history. It also displays original statuary from the Hôtel de Ville. The art collection includes works by Pieter Bruegel the Elder and Peter Paul Rubens, but the biggest attraction is the display of some 800 ornate costumes worn by that naughty little Brussels mascot, the Manneken-Pis statue *(see page 35)*, on the top floor.

Three narrow guild houses sit beside the Maison du Roi. No. 28, **La Chambrette de l'Amman** (House of the Amman), was the house of the duke's representative on the

Town Council in medieval times. The middle house, **Le Pigeon**, was home to Victor Hugo in 1851. **La Chaloupe d'Or** (Golden Longboat, 1697) is easily recognisable; it is topped by a statue of St Boniface. Originally the House of the Tailors, it is also now a café.

On the eastern side of the square, you will find **La Maison des Ducs de Brabant** (House of the Dukes of Brabant). This façade of harmonious design is in fact six houses and is named for the figures decorating it rather than its former owners.

Three houses lead back towards the Hôtel de Ville. **L'Arbre d'Or** (Golden Tree) at No. 10 is the House of the Brewers – look for gilded emblems of hops and wheat – and has a small museum of brewing, the **Musée de la Brasserie** (open Apr–Nov daily 10am–5pm; Dec–Mar Sat–Sun noon–5pm; admission fee). A refreshing beer is included in the admission price. **Le Cygne** (The Swan), next door at No. 9, is now one of the best restaurants in the city. Originally, it housed the butcher's guild before becoming a tavern and surrogate home to political theorists Karl Marx and Friedrich Engels. It was here in 1848 that they finalised the *Communist Manifesto*, though they had both made a promise not to become involved in politics when they were offered asylum in Belgium. **L'Etoile** (The Star) completes the vista. This house, the smallest on the square, was knocked down when rue Charles Buls was widened and replaced with a second floor supported by arcades. Below the arcades you'll find a reclining bronze statue of **Everard 't Serclaes**, depicted in the throes of death. He was

The sign for Le Cygne

Musée du Costume

murdered in 1388 for defending Brussels against powerful ducal enemies. This effigy is considered to bring continued good luck to the people of the city. Rub his arm and the nose of his dog to ensure your share of good fortune.

L'Ilot Sacré

The Grand-Place is surrounded by a medieval warren of narrow streets. Their names tell of the activities that took place here in days gone by: Marché-aux-Fromages (Cheese Market), Marché-aux-Herbes (Herb and Grass Market) and Marché-aux Poulets (Chicken Market). This really was the commercial heart of the city. At the beginning of the 19th century, the area was cut by wide boulevards, created when the River Senne was culverted and arcaded (see page 14). The name l'Ilot Sacré or the Sacred Isle was conjured up to protect it from redevelopment in the 20th century.

One street south of Grand-Place is rue Violette, home to the **Musée du Costume et de la Dentelle** (Costume and Lace Museum; open Mon–Tues and Thur–Fri 10am–12.30pm and 1.30–5pm, Sat–Sun 2–5pm; admission fee). Two 18th-century brick gabled houses provide the backdrop to a fine collection of Belgian fashions and lace from the 19th and 20th centuries. Further south, at the corner of rue de l'Etuve and rue du Chêne, is Brussels' most famous statue, the **Manneken-Pis** (see box, right).

North of the Grand-Place you can stroll through the **Galeries Royales St-Hubert**. Completed in 1847 this beautiful shopping arcade (in fact three separate, but connected arcades) was one of the first of its kind in Europe; nowadays, it features the best in Brussels' labels. Beautiful glass ceilings allow light to flood the walkways. The Galeries intersect rue des Bouchers, a pedestrian-only street peppered with restaurants and one of the most atmospheric places in which to eat on a summer evening.

Taking the western route out of the Grand-Place along rue au Beurre (Butter Street), look out for the Dandoy shop on your left. This family-run business, started in 1829, is a Brussels institution. Stop by for delicious marzipan and *speculoos* biscuits before you start your itinerary, and, in summer, try the refreshing ice cream. At the end of rue au Beurre, you will find the rear façade of the ornate **Bourse** (Stock Exchange) directly ahead. A relatively recent Brussels monument, it was completed in 1873 on the site of a former convent.

In a busy part of town, the adjacent 11th-century Romanesque **Église St-Nicolas** (Church of St Nicholas) is a quietly

Manneken-Pis

Why are large crowds always gathered at the corner of rue de l'Etuve and rue du Chêne? There are almost more cameras here than at a Hollywood premiere. This is the site of Manneken-Pis, the irreverent little statue whose method of delivering water to the fountain below embodies the somewhat offbeat attitude of the average native *Bruxellois*.

The tiny chap is renowned for his wardrobe of around 800 suits – the first one was a gift from the Elector of Bavaria in 1698 – though you may find him naked when you visit. He has been kidnapped three times: once in 1745 by the English, and again in 1747 by the French. On the third and last occasion, in 1817, Manneken-Pis was found broken in pieces. In fact, the statue you see today is a replica of one that was fashioned from the fragments.

Scientastic

Bourse metro station plays host to **Scientastic** (open school days 10am–5.30pm, Sat–Sun and school holidays 2–5.30pm; <www.scientastic.be>; admission fee). This is an interactive attraction where visitors can learn all about the world of science through hands-on experiments, tricks and illusions. It's great for children of all ages.

spiritual oasis. Refurbished in Gothic style in the 14th century and rebuilt several times since, the little church still shows traces of its original rough construction.

Some years ago, remains of 13th-century Brussels were discovered beneath rue de la Bourse and excavated by archaeologists. The site has been designated the **Bruxella 1238 Museum** (guided visits only, 1st Wed of month 10.15am in English, and by advance reservation, tel: 02-279 4355; admission fee) and offers a fascinating view of the city's early development. The main entrance of the Bourse sits on boulevard Anspach, a wide street created after the River Senne was tamed (see page 14).

Place de la Monnaie to Place de Brouckère

To the north of the Bourse is **place de la Monniae**, where the Belgian Revolution started in 1830 – crowds rushed out of the **Théâtre Royal de la Monnaie** after hearing the opera La Muette de Portici. **Place des Martyrs**, just a little way north, commemorates those who died in the fight for independence in 1830. The restored buildings are in the neo-Classical style and were constructed in the 1770s, though a number of monuments were added in the 1870s and 1880s. You can reach the square by going along rue Neuve, a busy shopping street.

From place de la Monniae, it is only a short walk to **place de Brouckère**, created in the late 1800s as a homage to the grand squares of Paris. Mayor Jules Anspach wanted his city to rival the French capital and held a competition to make sure the buildings on the square were the finest possible. Today, many have been replaced by more modern structures and those that remain are somewhat lost in a sea of neon. Place de Brouckère is one of the city's entertainment centres, and the terrace café of the Métropole hotel is one of the places to see and be seen.

The Cathedral

The **Cathédrale des Sts-Michel-et-Gudule** (open Mon–Fri 8am–6pm, Sat–Sun 8.30am–6pm; <www.kathedraalst michiel.be>; cathedral free; admission fee to crypt, treasury and archaeological zone) is a few minutes' walk to the northeast of the Grand-Place. The cathedral was founded as a church in 1047, dedicated to the Archangel Michael. Gudule was a saint from Flanders, and her relics were kept in the chapel at St-Géry until being transferred here. The choir dates from the 13th century, and the nave was added in the 14th century. The church gained cathedral status in 1962.

Sts-Michel-et-Gudule interior

The approach to the cathedral has been landscaped, and a flight of steps was added in 1860 to make the most of the views of the 15th-century façade. The twin towers are by Jan van Ruysbroeck, who also designed the tower on the Town

Hall. Stained-glass windows depict members of the Burgundian and Spanish ruling families, along with biblical scenes. Above the choir are five windows depicting Louis II and his wife Marie of Habsburg, while the windows of the northern transept show Charles V and his wife Isabella of Portugal. A number of royals, including Charles of Lorraine, are buried in the chancel. The pulpit is perhaps the most ornate element in the cathedral. The depiction of Adam and Eve being driven from the Garden of Eden was carved in 1699 by Hendrik Verbruggen of Antwerp. Below ground are the remains of two towers (*c.*1200), corners of the original church dating from the 10th century, which were discovered in the 1980s.

Comic Strip Centre

On the northern outskirts of l'Ilot Sacré, on rue des Sables, is a museum commemorating Belgium's immense contribu-

Inside the Centre Belge de la Bande-Dessinée

tion to the development of the comic strip as an art form. The **Centre Belge de la Bande-Dessinée** (Belgian Comic Strip Centre; Tues–Sun 10am–6pm; <www.cbbd.be>; admission

> ### Hergé
>
> The actual name of Tintin's creator was Georges Rémi. Hergé is the French pronunciation of his initials rendered in reverse.

fee) acts as a resource centre for studies into the genre and has exhibits that bring these comic book and celluloid heroes to life, with *Tintin* and his inventor Hergé taking pride of place. The museum is housed in the Art Nouveau former Waucquez department store, designed and built by Victor Horta in 1906, and faithfully restored.

THE LOWER CITY

West of the Bourse, the Lower City has seen many changes over the last 1,000 years. In the 13th century, a large community of *béguines* (religious lay women) was established in the Convent of Notre-Dame de la Vigne. The women found safety in the order, living in a large walled compound. The compound was ransacked and abolished during the French Revolution, and now only the **Église St-Jean-Baptiste-au-Béguinage** remains.

Boulevard Anspach separates the Ilot Sacré from the oldest areas of the city, centred on the marketplace at **place St-Géry**. The fine covered market hall (1881) in the square is now an arts centre, surrounded by bars and restaurants.

Following the completion of the Willebroeck Canal between Brussels and Antwerp in 1561, goods could be transported to the city by water. Quays built in what is now the Marché-aux-Poissons (Fish Market) have since been filled in, but the street names still relate to their original purposes: quai aux Briques (bricks) and quai au Bois-à-Brûler (firewood), for

Church of St-Jacques

example. The most central quay reaches as far as place Ste-Catherine with **Église Ste-Catherine** at its centre. This church originates in the 14th century but was rebuilt in 1854. The square is also the location of the Tour Noire (Black Tower), one of the few remains of the original city wall.

PLACE ROYALE

While the commercial town grew on marshy ground, the families with power lived on Coudenberg (Cold Hill). Today, this part of town still has palaces, and is home to some of the city's major museums. To reach the museums, take a route east from the Grand-Place through the ornamental gardens of the **Mont des Arts**, passing the statues of King Albert I and his wife Queen Elisabeth facing each other across place de l'Albertine. The Monts des Arts complex was a contentious redevelopment. It was a project to create a centre of arts and learning backed by Leopold II, but resulted in the destruction of a large residential area in the 1890s. Unfortunately, before the rebuilding began, Leopold died, and the project foundered. A large garden area was a temporary solution that lasted until after World War II. The building of the **Royal Library** in 1954 and the public records office (begun in 1960) have encased the remaining gardens in stone and concrete.

Once through the gardens, there is a view up to **place Royale**, decorated with a statue of Godefroid de Bouillon, a crusader and ruler of Jerusalem. Behind this you will see the campanile of the **church of St-Jacques-sur-Coudenberg**. This part of the capital was changed greatly by Charles of Lorraine when he became governor of the Low Countries in the mid-1700s. He looked towards Vienna for inspiration and brought together the then-disparate architectural styles of Coudenberg to create a unified ensemble. The **Musée du XVIIIe Siècle** can be seen in place du Musée in the Louis XVI Palais de Charles de Lorraine (open Wed, Sat 1–5pm; admission fee), though Charles died before it was completed. The apartments bear witness to the Habsburg love of luxury.

As you walk towards place Royale you'll see a splendid Art Nouveau building on your left. This is the **Old England Department Store**, designed in 1899 by Paul Saintenoy. The building now houses the **Musée des Instruments de Musique** (Musical Instruments Museum; open Tues–Fri 9.30am–5pm, Sat–Sun 10am–5pm; <www.mimfgov.be>; admission fee). The museum is a treasure trove of musical instruments, displaying over 1,500 in 90 groups relating to type and age. On entering, you receive headphones that allow you to listen to a selection of music at each site.

Antique keyboard

Art Museums

From Place Royale, it is easy to see Charles of Lorraine's vision for the area. Turning right down rue de la Régence, on your immediate right are the **Musées Royaux des Beaux-Arts de Belgique**

(Royal Museums of Fine Arts; open Tues–Sun 10am–5pm; <www.fine-arts-museum.be>; admission fee), including both historical and modern art. This is one of the finest collections in Europe, started at the behest of Napoleon Bonaparte. It moved into its present location in the court rooms of Charles' palace in 1887. The museum has been updated and thoughtfully designed, with large open halls for relaxed viewing. Even so, the collection takes a long time to see, so take advantage of the on-site café for refreshment if you become tired.

The **Musée d'Art Ancien** (Museum of Historical Art) offers more than 1,200 canvasses, with a wealth of Flemish masters on show. Works by Dirk Bouts (1420–75) and Hans Memling (1439–94) showcase the 1400s, with Memling's *La Vierge et l'Enfant* being particularly notable. Hieronymus Bosch (*c.*1450–1516) and Gerard David (*c.*1460–1523) lead into the 1500s. Pieter Bruegel (1527–69), whose realism had a profound influence on art within the Low Countries, is also represented, along with Peter Paul Rubens (1577–1640) and his pupil Antony van Dyck (1599–1641). Works by Dutch artists Frans Hals (born in Antwerp) and Rembrandt are featured, too. In addition, the museum devotes space to the artistic movements that developed at the end of the 19th century, such as Impressionism – the collection includes paintings by Renoir, Monet and Sisley.

The **Musée d'Art Moderne** (Modern Art Museum) concentrates on pieces from the late 19th and 20th centuries. Though you enter through a neo-Classical building, part of the museum is, in fact, built below ground level with a huge central glass wall allowing light into the galleries. Cubist, Fauvist, Abstract and Surrealist artists are represented. The pieces are arranged chronologically and feature Belgian artists such as René Magritte (1898–1967), Rik Wouters (1882–1916) and Paul Delvaux (1897–1994), along with work by Picasso, Dalí, Miró, Gauguin and Seurat.

Parc de Bruxelles and Palais Royal

On the south side of the museum is a small sculpture garden; however, if you head north from the museum entrance back across the square, you will see the trees of the **Parc de Bruxelles** ahead. Originally a hunting preserve of the dukes of Brabant, it has been open land for several centuries. The formal park with ornamental fountains and statuary in the French style was completed in 1835.

On its south side, the garden looks on to the impressive front façade of the **Palais Royal** (Royal Palace), once part of the site of the Palace of the Dukes of Brabant. Construction began in 1820 following a fire, which destroyed the previous building. It was greatly modified under Leopold II during his reign (1865–1909), with several of the chambers and the façade given Classical and Louis XVI-style embellishments. The palace is now used for ceremonial occasions, as the royal

When the flag flies over the Palais Royal, the king is in residence family lives at Laeken Palace on the northern outskirts of the city. If the king is in residence, you will see the Belgian flag fluttering on the flagpole above the entrance.

The palace is open for tours from the end of July to the beginning of September, but if you want to know more about the Belgian royal family, visit the **Musée BELvue** (open June–Sept Tues–Sun 10am–6pm; Oct–May Tues–Sun 10am–5pm; <www.belvue.be>; admission fee), which is housed in the Bellevue Apartments in the east wing of the palace. The rooms still retain their original splendour. Tasteful exhibits have been added to tell the story of each royal reign in chronological order, including both the personal and professional lives of the monarchs. Artefacts include personal belongings and photographs of the royal family. There is also a memorial to King Baudouin, who died in 1993.

On the opposite side of the Parc de Bruxelles is the **Palais de la Nation**, which was constructed in 1783. It has been the seat of the Belgian government since 1830.

Travel back towards the old part of the city via rue Baron Horta and you will find **BOZAR (Palais des Beaux-Arts)** on the corner to your left, on rue Ravenstein. Completed in 1928 to a design by Victor Horta, it is greatly admired for its interior detail. Major cultural events such as the Queen Elisabeth Music Contests are held here; temporary exhibitions take place in the foyer, so something is always happening. Also on rue Baron Horta, the **Musée du Cinéma** (open Fri–Wed from 5.30pm, Thur from 2.30pm; admission fee) has daily screenings.

Congress Column

The Colonne du Congrès (Congress Column), on rue Royale, commemorates Belgium's Independence Revolution in 1830. Atop its 47-m (153-ft) shaft stands a statue of King Leopold I (1790–1865). At its base is the Tomb of the Unknown Soldier.

LE SABLON

Once a marshy wasteland, this part of Brussels saw mansions built for the ruling families in the 16th century, but became especially fashionable in the 19th century. Many fine town houses date from this time. Today, it has numerous antiques shops, art galleries, good restaurants and busy bars, which makes it a popular place to browse and have lunch.

Guild statue in place du Petit-Sablon

It is easy to find the Sablon from the Musée des Beaux-Arts area. A short walk south along rue de la Régence brings you to the church of **Notre-Dame du Sablon** (open Mon–Fri 9am–5pm, Sat–Sun 10am–6.30pm; free) at the top of **place du Grand-Sablon**. The church was built in 1304 by the guild of crossbowmen, and the statue of Our Lady here is said to have healing properties. The church has undergone several extensions and embellishments, the last in the 19th century. Since the 15th century, the square in the shadow of the church has hosted markets. It is still home to an antiques market every weekend.

Behind the church and across rue de la Régence is **place du Petit-Sablon** (open Mon–Fri 9am–5pm, Sat–Sun 10am–6.30pm; free), with its own park, laid out in 1890. It is decorated with historically significant statuary. Each post of the wrought-iron fence around the park is topped with the bronze figure of a man portraying a trade guild. Pride of place within the park is taken by a large sculptured tribute to counts Hornes and Egmont, who were beheaded in the Grand-Place in 1568 following unsuccessful protests against the excesses of Spanish rule. Beyond the square you'll see the **Palais d'Egmont** (1534), once the family home of the Dukes of Egmont, but now housing part of the Belgian Ministry of Foreign Affairs. You can't tour the palace, but you can enjoy the gardens.

LES MAROLLES

Les Marolles is a working-class district that grew on trade and labour skills – coopering and blacksmithing, primarily. The Marolles has never been gentrified (though in recent years this has begun around its edges) and retains a unique atmosphere, its streets filled with hustle and bustle.

Overlooking the whole area is the **Palais de Justice**, a huge edifice that became a *cause célèbre* when its plans were revealed. It was one of the largest buildings in Europe when it was completed in 1883, and a large piece of the Marolles had to be demolished to make way for it – much to the chagrin of the local people. Everything about the building is on a grand scale, including an entrance porch 42m (150ft) in height.

The rest of the Marolles spreads out to the west and is cut by two main streets. **Rue Haute** is the longest street in the Brussels *commune*, and one of the oldest. The artist Pieter Bruegel the Elder lived from 1562 in a house at No. 132 that can be dated from earlier that century. Bruegel and other members of his family are buried in **Notre-Dame de la Chapelle** (open Mon–Fri 9.30am–4.30pm, Sat 12.30– 5pm, Sun 8am–7.30pm; free) at the city end of rue Haute. Consecrated in 1210, the church underwent renovations in 1421 following a fire, and the Baroque belltower was added after the bombardment of 1695 destroyed an earlier tower. The

Flea market at place du Jeu-de-Balle

interior has several fine works, the best being the memorial to Bruegel (the Elder) by his son Jan. At the *petite ceinture* end of rue Haute, you will find the **Porte de Hal**, the last remaining medieval city gate, saved from destruction because it served as a prison. Built in the 14th century, it was radically altered in the 19th century in the faux-medieval fashion of the day – most of the top embellishments date from this time. The lower original walls have a much simpler design.

The second major street of the Marolles is rue Blaes, which is famed for its flea market (daily 7am–2pm) at **place du Jeu-de-Balle**. You can buy almost anything here, from furniture and clothes to old 78 records and family photographs. The streets surrounding place du Jeu-de-Balle are dotted with numerous cafés and bars, as well as lots of secondhand stores. Look out for De Skieven Architek, a bar on the square whose name sums up what the people thought of the designer of the Palais de Justice.

BEYOND THE OLD CITY

There are numerous attractions to visit outside the old town and within the other *communes* of the city. Some can be reached on foot, the rest by public transport.

To the East

The area directly east of the old town has perhaps seen the most change in the last 50 years. This area is the heart of the European Union administration, with numerous office buildings housing EU departments, support staff and the diplomatic missions and pressure groups aiming to influence the EU's decisions. As much as 1.2 sq km (0.46 sq miles) of space is taken by the various arms of this one institution.

The **European Parliament** building is at l'Espace Léopold. (It is often derisively called the *Caprice des Dieux* by Belgians, because of the building's resemblance to the box in which the cheese of the same name is packed.) Its curved glass roof rising to 70m (228ft) can be seen from all around this district, and there are particularly pretty views from **Parc Léopold** at its eastern side.

South of the park you will find the **Institut des Sciences Naturelles** (Natural Sciences Institute). Its museum (open Tues–Fri 9.30am–4.45pm, Sat–Sun and school holidays, except July–Aug, 10am–6pm; <www.sciencesnaturelles.be>; admission fee) aims to enhance understanding of the natural world, and is best known for its dinosaur collection, particularly a group of more than 30 iguanadons found in southern Belgium in 1905. Several have been reconstructed in upright positions, while others are displayed as they were found.

Just a little way further east from the European headquarters is the **Parc du Cinquantenaire**. When Belgium reached its Golden Jubilee, King Leopold II wanted to celebrate by creating a monument to national pride. He enlisted the help of

Triumphal arch at Parc du Cinquantenaire

architect Gédéon Bordiau who planned a grand esplanade, formal gardens and a ceremonial arch, with two wings to house museum and gallery space. However, the project hit snags and was not complete for the celebrations. The monumental arch, which features a large bronze *quadriga* sculpture entitled *Brabant Raising the National Flag*, was completed in 1888, but the complex was since hit by fire, and one of the wings has been completely rebuilt in a slightly different style. Today the Cinquantenaire complex houses three museums. It is easily reached by metro to Mérode station.

The south wing is home to the **Musée du Cinquantenaire** (open Tues–Fri 9.30am–5pm; Sat–Sun 10am–5pm; <www.kmkg-mrah.be>; admission fee), a collection of art and historical artefacts that ranges from prehistoric times to the present. The Roman and Greek remains are particularly fine, with beautiful mosaics and statuary. Rooms dedicated to earlier Near Eastern civilisation, and ancient Asian and American

Musée du Cinquantenaire

societies are also impressive. Religious relics, furniture, pottery and jewellery are all of exceptionally high quality. There are over 140 rooms to explore here, so the map given to you at reception is absolutely vital.

In the south hall next door is **Autoworld** (open Apr–Sept daily 10am–6pm; Oct–Mar Mon–Fri 10am–5pm, Sat–Sun 10am–6pm; <www.autoworld.be>; admission fee), a collection of over 450 vehicles. Many early Belgian car makers are represented, with a number of pre-1920 Minerva cars and a 1948 Imperia, the last Belgian car produced before production was swallowed by larger European manufacturers. Almost every maker is represented, including Rolls-Royce, Studebaker and Mercedes.

The **Musée Royal de l'Armée et d'Histoire Militaire** (Army and Military History Museum; open Tues–Sun 9am–noon and 1–4.45pm; <www.klm-mra.be>; free) is in the north wing and hall. One of the largest museums of its kind in the world, it covers 10 centuries of military history. In the 19th-century section are uniforms, arms and the personal effects of soldiers from Belgian units, including those of Leopold I. The walls are filled with images of uniformed gentlemen, and shot-torn battle flags hang from the ceiling. Another section features 14th- and 15th-century artefacts, with suits of armour, swords and shields. There are displays of tanks and other vehicles, and an aircraft section including a Spitfire and Hurricane from World War II.

To the South

Avenue Louise, leading southeast from the *petite ceinture,* has cafés, restaurants, department stores and *haute couture* boutiques. There are several Art Nouveau homes on the adjacent residential streets, including the **Musée Horta** (Horta Museum; open Tues–Sun 2–5.30pm; <www.hortamuseum. be>; admission fee) on rue Américaine. The building was designed by Victor Horta as a home and studio. It is considered to be the epitome of Art Nouveau architecture in Brussels.

Travelling to the end of avenue Louise (by tram from the Palais de Justice) leads you to the **Bois de la Cambre,** a park with lakes and pleasant paths for walking. Just before the park is the former Cistercian **Abbaye de la Cambre** (La

Art Nouveau

For all the demolition of architectural gems in recent decades, the tide seems to be turning towards preserving what remains of a remarkable heritage. And despite being the capital of so many other things, Brussels is perhaps proudest of being the 'capital of Art Nouveau', having been bequeathed some of the finest architecture of this exuberant turn-of-the-20th-century style. Property 'developers' and local government connivance have conspired to destroy some buildings, but others remain to dazzle the eye.

The foremost proponent of Art Nouveau, a style typified by naturalistic forms and motifs, was the Brussels architect Victor Horta, some of whose students continued the tradition. Notable examples of the genre are the Solvay Mansion, the cafés De Ultieme Hallucinatie and Le Falstaff, Magasins Waucquez department store (which houses the Belgian Comic Strip Centre), the Old England department store (which houses the Museum of Musical Instruments), the Tassel House, the florist De Baecker, and townhouses in square Ambiorix and square Marie-Louise.

Cambre Abbey), surrounded by an ornamental garden containing fountains and pools and the 13th-century church of **Notre-Dame de la Cambre**. The abbey buildings now house an art school and the National Geographical Institute. The *bois* itself is, in fact, the manicured tip of the **Forêt de Soignes**, Europe's largest beech forest.

To the West

West of the heart of Brussels is the *commune* of **Anderlecht**. One of the greatest men of the Renaissance, Desiderius Erasmus (1469–1536), lived here in a house dating in part from 1468. **Maison d'Erasme** (House of Erasmus; open Tues–Sun

House of Erasmus

10am–5pm; <www.erasmus house.museum>; admission fee) is a fine example of 15th-century architecture and features the desk of the philosopher, a Catholic contemporary of Martin Luther, who railed against the strictures of Catholic dogma. The upper floor has books and manuscripts relating to the humanist movement and religious strife. The Renaissance room is home to paintings by Hieronymus Bosch and Dirk Bouts. Across the street is the **Béguinage d'Anderlecht** (open Tues–Sun 10am–noon and 2–5pm; admission fee), founded in 1252. Two cottages housing a folklore museum can be visited.

To the North

Just beyond the *petite ceinture* in the north is the redeveloped Gare du Nord zone, which has attracted a number of hotels and bars and a lot of nightlife to the area. **Place Rogier**, home to restaurants, clubs and shopping malls, is the centre of the activity.

Beer museum

Situated close to the Béguinage d'Anderlecht, in a family-owned brewery in rue Gheude, the Musée Bruxellois de la Gueuze (open Mon–Fri 10am–5pm, Sat 10am–6pm; <www.cantillon.be>; admission fee) celebrates traditional Brussels beers. Perfect on a hot summer's day.

Going west from here leads you to the **Basilique Nationale du Sacré-Coeur** (National Basilica of the Sacred Heart), in Koekelberg. Begun in 1905 and completed in 1970, this church looks something like a modern take on a Byzantine basilica. A gallery in the dome affords panoramic views.

A short walk east from place Rogier is **Le Botanique**, a former botanical garden and glass house of 1826, which was transformed into a cultural centre in the 1980s. The interior is spectacular, with the glass houses – complete with plants – forming a link between the exhibition halls (these host theatre and musical events and temporary exhibitions).

Heysel

In 1935 and 1958, Brussels hosted major international exhibitions. The events were held in the north of the city at **Heysel**, where vast exhibition halls were built. Since that time, a number of attractions have developed here. All these can be accessed from the Heysel metro station.

The **Parc des Expositions** is a fine building erected for the 1935 exhibition. However, it is a structure from the 1958 World Fair that captured the hearts of the people and became one of the most popular symbols of Brussels. The

▶ recently refurbished **Atomium** (open daily 10am–6pm; <www.atomium.be>; admission fee) was built in the shape of the atomic structure of an iron crystal on a scale of 1:165 billion. Constructed of metal spheres linked by tubes, it was created to symbolise the great advances made in the sciences throughout the 20th century. There is a good view of Brussels and the surrounding countryside from the top sphere, a lofty 102m (332ft) high.

The Atomium is adjacent to **Bruparck**, a large recreational area filled with a variety of activities. Try **l'Océade** for water-based relaxation, or **Kinepolis** with its 26 cinemas showing the latest releases. **Mini-Europe** (open late Mar–June and Sept daily 9.30am–6pm; July–Aug daily 9.30am– 8pm (late July–end Aug Sat–Sun 9.30am–midnight); Oct– Dec and 1st week Jan 10am–6pm; <www.minieurope.com>; admission fee) celebrates European union in a light-hearted way. More than 300 of Europe's best-known landmarks have been recreated here in miniature (1:25 scale). You can visit a 4-m (13-ft) high Big Ben and a 13-m (42-ft) high Eiffel Tower – and press a button that causes the miniature Mount Vesuvius to erupt.

The Royal Estate at Laeken

South of Heysel is the **Domaine Royal de Laeken**, a vast estate and palace, where the royal family has residences. Although the palace is not open to the public, the magnificent **Serres Royales** (Royal Glass Houses) can be visited during three weeks in April or May. These were built at the behest of Leopold II following his visit to the Crystal Palace in London and other new glass houses of Europe. A monument to this monarch has been erected in the parc de Laeken opposite the palace. Leopold was enthusiastic about architectural styles and building methods – a passion that resulted in the construction of two Asian-inspired structures to the north of the palace. The **Pavillon Chinois** (Chinese Pavilion), with a carved wooden façade imported from Shanghai, was completed after Leopold's death in 1910. The pavilion now houses a collection of Chinese ceramics. The **Tour Japonaise** (Japanese Tower), reached by tunnel from the Chinese Pavilion, was designed and built by Parisian architect Alexandre Marcel. It is now used for exhibitions of antique Asian ceramics. The nearby former storeroom and workshop for the Chinese Pavilion has been renovated and opened as the **Musée d'Art Japonais** (Museum of Japanese Art), and together the three buildings now constitute the **Musées d'Extrême-Orient** (Museums of the Far East; open Tues–Fri 9.30am–5pm, Sat–Sun 10am–5pm; <www.kmkg-mrah.be>; admission fee).

In nearby Jette, a house on rue Esseghem was home to René Magritte from 1930 to 1954. The **Musée René Magritte** (open Wed–Sun 10am–6pm; <www.magrittemuseum.be>; admission fee) promotes the Surrealist painter's work.

The Chinese Pavilion at Laeken with a façade from Shanghai

ENVIRONS OF BRUSSELS

Tervuren

You can reach the suburban Flemish village of **Tervuren** by taking tram 44 from Montgomery metro station. The route takes you through the commune of **Woluwe-St-Lambert**, a pretty residential suburb with beautiful parks. It also plays host to the **Musée du Transport Urbain Bruxellois** (Brussels Urban Transport Museum; the museum is closed for renovation during 2007 and 2008; <www.trammuseumbrussels.be>; admission fee), directly on the public transport route, for those who enjoy old trams and trolley buses.

Belgian writer Roger Martin du Gard nicknamed Tervuren 'the Versailles of Belgium', and the royal estate here is based on Classical French architectural style and garden design.

Gardens surround the Musée Royal de l'Afrique Centrale

In 1897, Leopold II organised a colonial exhibition relating to his expanding lands in the Congo. This proved so successful that a permanent home was built for the exhibits, and an anthropological research centre was instituted. Leopold personally contracted Frenchman Charles Girault, designer of the Petit Palais in Paris, to build the museum. The **Musée Royal de l'Afrique Centrale/Koninklijk Museum voor Midden Afrika** (Royal Museum of Central Africa; open Tues–Fri 10am–5pm, Sat–Sun 10am–6pm; <www.africamuseum.be>; admission fee) on Leuvensesteenweg is a stunning building surrounded by acres of formal gardens. The exhibits include rather outdated displays of stuffed animals and a collection of species of insects that children seem to find fascinating. The museum also holds a fine collection of artefacts from central Africa, including weapons, musical instruments and ceremonial masks. The history of the exploration of Africa is covered, including the issue of slavery. Personal effects of David Livingstone and Henry Morton Stanley are included in this section. It also covers contemporary issues, such as desertification.

The formal gardens surrounding the museum give way to natural forest and parkland. There is a boating lake with lots of bird life, making Tervuren a relaxing spot on a sunny day.

Waterloo

Of the many battles that have taken place on Belgian soil, the Battle of **Waterloo** was one of the most important. Its impact on European history was long lasting and it proved to be the final rally for Napoleon in his unsuccessful bid to retake France's leadership. It was during June 1815 that a combined force from Britain, the Low Countries and Prussia began the campaign that would finally destroy the French Emperor. The armies met outside the village of Waterloo on 18 June. By the day's close the French had been routed, and nearly 50,000 men lay dead or wounded on the battlefield.

The Lion Mound at Waterloo

Travelling to the site today, one can still see how beautiful the countryside must have been. It has changed with the addition of a modern four-lane highway (the Brussels outer ring road). However, many of the historic buildings have been preserved as museums devoted to the battle. **La Butte de Lion** (Lion Mound), built on the site in 1826 by the government of the Netherlands, marks the spot where their leader, the Prince of Orange, was wounded. The 40-m (132-ft) mound is topped by a cast iron statue of a lion 4.5m (14ft) in height.

At the base of the mound is a **Visitors' Centre** (Butte de Lion, Visitors' Centre, Panorama and Waxworks Museum open Apr–Oct daily 9.30am–6.30pm; Nov–Mar daily 10am–5pm; <www.culturespaces.com/waterloo>; separate or combined admission fee; visitors' centre free), which presents an audio-visual exhibit of the battle, including the tactics and movements of the opposing forces and a time frame. Nearby, in a separate building, is the **Panorama de la Bataille** (Panorama of the Battle), a 110m-by-12m (358ft-by-39ft) circular painting executed by Louis Dumoulin in 1913 and depicting scenes of one of the most important events of the battle. Across the road is the **Musée des Cires** (Waxworks Museum), containing waxworks of the leading military figures involved in the combat.

Strolling around the battlefield, you'll pass the fortified farms of Hougoumont and La Haie-Sainte, which played crucial roles in the battle. At the southern end of the battlefield is the **Dernier Quartier Général de Napoléon** (Napoleon's Last Headquarters; open Apr–Sept daily 10am–6.30pm; Oct–Mar daily 1–6.30pm; admission fee), housed in what was la Ferme du Caillou (Caillou Farm), where Napoleon had his headquarters on the eve of the battle. There are a few pieces of memorabilia, including the skeleton of a hussar found at the site.

The British Duke of Wellington had his headquarters at the inn in the village of Waterloo 4km (2½ miles) to the north. Restored in 1975, it is now home to the **Musée Wellington** (Wellington Museum; open Apr–Sept 9.30am–6.30pm; Oct–Mar 10am–5pm; <www.museewellington.be>; admission fee), which also has a section depicting the history of Waterloo itself. There is a room devoted to the duke, containing numerous personal effects. Other rooms are given over to the Dutch and Prussian armies, and maps of the battlefield.

Battle of Waterloo

One of many surprising aspects of the Battle of Waterloo is that it did not take place at Waterloo at all, but in rolling fields 4km (2½ miles) further south, where the road from Brussels, after passing through the Forêt de Soignes and Waterloo, arrives at a low ridge beyond the farm of Mont Saint-Jean. A traveller taking this route on 18 June 1815 would have run into the French Emperor Napoleon Bonaparte and his 75,000 troops here, doing their headlong best to go in the opposite direction.

More surprising by far is that Napoleon, who won an empire through his supreme grasp of the military art, lost it in the end by putting his head down and charging repeatedly uphill in vain, bloody attempts to shift the Duke of Wellington's 72,000-man army blocking the road to Brussels. 'If my orders are properly executed,' Napoleon told his generals before kicking off the carnage, 'we will sleep tonight in Brussels.' The superb courage of the French soldiers came near to confirming their emperor's prediction. Wellington called the contest 'the nearest run thing you ever saw in your life'.

EXCURSIONS

Antwerp

Where Brussels has developed into Belgium's most important administrative and legislative city, Antwerp (Antwerpen/Anvers), only 48km (30 miles) to the north, has long been the country's commercial heart. Founded on the River Scheldt (or Schelde), it was an important staging post on the route from England into central Europe and developed into an important trading port by the late Middle Ages. During the Renaissance, Antwerp was one of the cultural capitals of Europe, with the artist Peter Paul Rubens greatly influencing his native town, and philosopher/businessman Christophe Plantin acting as a magnet for advocates of the new sciences.

Walking along the streets of Antwerp today, you quickly become aware of a different atmosphere than that in Brussels. There is a raw energy here, an activity of movement of cargo and goods rather than of paper or files. The city is still one of the largest ports in Europe and the world's centre of the diamond polishing industry.

It is impossible to miss the **Onze-Lieve-Vrouwe-kathedraal** (Cathedral of Our Lady; open Mon–Fri 10am–5pm, Sat and the day before a religious holiday 10am–3pm, Sun 1–4pm; <www.dekathedraal.be>; admission fee), whose great steeple, at 123m (404ft), towers above every other building in the old town.

Diamond city

Antwerp is the world's centre for the diamond trade. Most of the cutting, polishing and trading takes place in the Diamond Quarter, where the offices of the Hoge Raad voor Diamant (Diamond High Council) and the Beurs voor Diamanthandel (Diamond Exchange) are located amid a glittering array of jewellery shops.

Built during the 14th and 15th centuries, it is a remarkable Gothic creation, the largest in Belgium, and its interior proportions almost take the breath away. Four Rubens masterpieces grace the cathedral: *Raising of the Cross* (1610), *Descent from the Cross* (1614), *Resurrection* (1612), and *Ascension of the Virgin* (1626) are colourful and dramatic canvasses that give full rein to the artist's prodigious talent. The largest of the cathedral's chapels, St Anthony's, has a beautiful stained-glass window, dating from 1503; it depicts King Henry VII of England

Cathedral of Our Lady

kneeling with his queen and was created to commemorate a commercial deal made at that time between England and the Low Countries.

A stroll around the outside of the cathedral also reveals a few surprises. The area acted as a commercial centre as well as a religious site and huddling around the base of the structure are buildings as old as the church. These are now cafés, bars and souvenir shops. Across from the cathedral, with an entrance at Oude Koornmarkt 16, Vlaeykensgang is a tranquil medieval courtyard. In front of the cathedral is the small **Handschoenmarkt** with its cafés. Look out for an ornate well, the **Putkevie**, topped by a statue of Brabo, Antwerp's hero.

Antwerp's Grote Markt, with the Brabo fountain at its centre

Walking west towards the river will bring you to the **Grote Markt** and the Stadhuis (Town Hall). This square, like the Grand-Place in Brussels, epitomises the power of trade and commerce throughout the history of the city. The mansions that line the Grote Markt were built for the trades' guilds or corporations, which wielded great power during Antwerp's heyday. The most ornate is No. 7, **De Oude Voetboog** (House of the Old Crossbow). At the centre of the Grote Markt is a 19th-century fountain, with a depiction of Brabo wielding the severed hand of the giant Antigoon *(see box, right)*.

Antwerp's Town Hall

The **Stadhuis** (Town Hall; guided tours Mon–Wed and Fri–Sat 11am, 2 and 3pm; admission fee) was built in the 1560s under Cornelis Floris de Vriendt. It has a sombre balance in its design, with lines of faux columns atop a ground floor of arched doorways. The central section, added in the 19th century, is Flemish in its architectural adornment. Coats of arms of local duchies grace the façade, and a central alcove displays a statute of Our Lady, the protector of the city. Inside, the corridors have dioramas depicting historical council meetings and activities in the chambers. To the south is **Groenplaats**, lined with shops and cafés and sporting a statue of Rubens.

After exploring Grote Markt, head towards the river via the Gothic **Vleeshuis** (Butchers' Hall). Built in the 16th century, it looks like a church with a fine façade and spires, but was a guild house and trading hall. When you reach the river, you can take a boat trip downstream to the busy modern harbour to watch cargoes being loaded and unloaded.

Boat trips leave regularly in summer from the dockside at the **Steen**. This 13th-century castle is the oldest remaining structure in Antwerp, and legend has it that it was the home of Antigoon the giant. It later became a prison. Today, it houses the **Nationaal Scheepvaartmuseum** (National Maritime Museum; open Tues–Sun 10am–5pm; admission fee), which has a large collection of maps and charts, navigation equipment and other sea-faring artefacts. Antwerp owes a great deal of its prosperity to the development of sea trade, and the museum is a fitting tribute to the merchant fleet.

Brabo – Antwerp's Hero

Legend tells of how the citizens of Antwerp were being terrorised by an evil giant, Antigoon, who extracted tolls from those who wanted to cross the river. If travellers could not pay, Antigoon would cut off their hands in punishment. Young Silvius Brabo, a relative of Julius Caesar, was brave enough to stand up to the monster and beat him, cutting off his hand as a sign of victory and throwing it into the River Scheldt. His heroics not only saved the whole town from tyranny, but may also have given the town its name – *hand werpen* (hand-throw).

Printing and Art

Rubens' *Education of the Virgin* in the Royal Fine Arts Museum

Walk south of Grote Markt towards the **Plantin-Moretus Museum** (open Tues–Sun 10am–5pm; <www.plantin-moretus.be>; admission fee) in Vrijdagmarkt. Christopher Plantin was one of the most important craftsmen-businessmen of the late Spanish Empire. His house and neighbouring printing press offer an insight into the man and the philosophy of this time of great expansion and learning, concentrating on writing and printing. Seven antique printing presses are still in working order, and there is a collection of rare manuscripts. Pride of place must go to the *Biblia Regia* (Polyglot Bible), printed between 1568 and 1572 in eight volumes in Hebrew, Syriac, Aramaic, Latin and Greek. Plantin's family sat for portraits that are displayed on the walls; many of the portraits were painted by Rubens.

More art can be found at the **Koninklijk Museum voor Schone Kunsten Antwerpen** (Royal Fine Arts Museum Antwerp; open Tues–Sat 10am–5pm, Sun 10am–6pm; <www.kmska.be>; admission fee) on Leopold de Waelplaats. The fine collection of Flemish art covers five centuries, with the master Rubens being well represented – his works include *Adoration of the Magi* and *St Francis of Assisi*. There are also many paintings by the Rubens school and Rubens' illustrious pupils, including Antoon van Dyck and Jacob Jordaens. Hans Memling, Dirk Bouts and another Antwerp master, Quentin Matsys, also have works here. A collection of beautiful art of the Rubens school can also be found in **Sint-Pauluskerk** (St Paul's Church; open May–Sept daily 2–5pm; free) on Sint-Paulusstraat. The church was part of a Dominican monastery and was constructed during the mid-16th century in the late-Gothic style. The interior is decorated with fine wood panelling surpassed only by the majesty of 15 large canvasses depicting the *Mysteries of the Rosaries*, painted by 11 different master painters.

Rubens House

The **Rubenshuis** (Rubens House; open Tues–Sun 10am–5pm; admission fee) at Wapper 9–11, located just off the main shopping street, Meir, is today surrounded by modern shops and cafés, although it still gives an impression of the immense wealth and influence of arguably the best-known Belgian artist. He used the money earned from painting portraits of European royalty to build a large and substantial home for his family – eight children by two wives – and a studio for himself in 1610. He must have been happy with the result, as he spent the last 30 years of his life here. The family lived in a Flemish-style wing of the house. It is austerely furnished, but look out for a self-portrait of the artist

Street performer

Inside Antwerp's Sint-Carolus Borromeuskerk

hanging in the dining room. Contrast this family wing with the studio, which was decorated in the then-fashionable Baroque style. Here you will find Rubens' extensive collection of Greek and Roman sculpture.

Rubens had a hand in the design and adornment of the 17th-century **Sint-Carolus Borromeuskerk** (St Charles Borromeo Church; open Mon–Sat 10am–12.30pm and 2–5pm; admission fee), in Hendrik Conscienceplein, east of the Grote Markt. The artist, along with members of his family, is buried in the **Sint-Jacobskerk** (St James's Church), inside which there are a number of his paintings, and a portrait of Rubens.

Works by Rubens are also in evidence in the **Mayer Van den Bergh Museum** (open Tues–Sun 10am–5pm; <www.mayervandenbergh.be>; admission fee) on Lange Gasthuisstraat, and although Pieter Bruegel was a resident of Brussels, there are several of his works here, including his earliest known painting, *Twelve Proverbs,* and his sombre view of war *Dulle Griet* (Mad Meg). The museum is based on the collection of Sir Fritz van den Bergh and includes a large collection of sculpture, tapestries and ceramics from the 12th to the 18th centuries, in addition to a wide range of art.

Museum of Modern Art

Known as MuHKA, the **Museum voor Hedendaagse Kunst Antwerpen** (Antwerp Museum of Modern Art; open Tues–Sun 10am–5pm; <www.muhka.be>; admission fee) occupies a former warehouse in Antwerp's old port, on Leuvenstraat, close to the Scheldt. Behind the warehouse's original Art Deco façade, a collection of cutting-edge Belgian and international art is expanding to fill the enormous interior.

In the newer part of town (*c.*19th century) across the ring road, a boulevard skirts the old town. Browse in the modern stores lining Meir, a pedestrian-only area. As Meir becomes Leystraat, the buildings take on a very ornate style, flanking Teniersplein with its statue of the artist David Tenier (a relative of Bruegel). Cross Frankrijklei and walk towards the railway station along Keyserlei. To your left is **De Vlaamse Opera** (Flemish Opera House), which opened in 1907.

Diamonds Galore

To the right of Keyserlei is the diamond district where 70 percent of the world's raw diamonds come to be graded, polished and set. This weighs in at 25 million carats each year. The streets here are filled with jewellery shops selling items from only a few euros to individual pieces worth hundreds of thousands. If you want to know more about this most precious of minerals, head to Diamondland in Appelmansstraat. This diamond showroom and polishing house features films and polishing exhibitions about the trade.

In the neighbourhood of Antwerp Centraal Station is the **Diamantkwartier** (Diamond Quarter), the centre of the city's diamond trade. The collection of the **Diamantmuseum Provincie Antwerpen** (Antwerp Province Diamond Museum; open May–Oct daily 10am–6pm; Nov–Dec and Feb–Apr 10am–5pm; <www.diamantmuseum.be>; admission fee) on Koningin Astridplein includes a reproduction of the Cullinan diamond, the largest ever found, from South Africa.

Antwerp Station was designed in French Renaissance style and opened in 1905. Its fine dome is reminiscent of a cathedral, and the station's proportions bear testament to the importance of investment in the rail industry at the end of the 19th century.

Beyond the station is **Antwerp Zoo** (open daily 10am–dusk; <www.zooantwerpen.be>; admission fee), founded in 1843 on 10 hectares (25 acres) of land.

Bruges

In the Middle Ages this small Belgian city, known as Brugge in Dutch, was one of the most influential in northern Europe, with a thriving economy based on trade with Europe and England. It was the leading city for textile and tapestry production and was a major trading town of the Baltic-based Hanseatic League. Cargoes of wool, furs and spices passed through its port, which was connected to the sea via the Zwin inlet. In 1384, the Burgundian leader Philip the Good made Bruges the capital of his growing kingdom, and artists Hans Memling and Jan van Eyck were at the centre of a royal court that was one of the most splendid in Europe. However, the city lost its influence as early

Along the canals

A tour through the canals of Bruges in an open boat is a delightful experience, and the view from this splendid vantage-point is memorable. All boats cover the same route and depart from several landing stages around the centre (Mar–Nov 10am–6pm; tour fee).

as the 15th century. Cheap textile imports from England flooded the market, and the Zwin inlet began to silt up. Bruges became land-locked and in time was all but forgotten.

However, it was this sudden loss of prestige and influence that has helped to make Bruges one of Europe's most popular tourist destinations. The town was never redeveloped, and today it still has an almost complete medieval historical area. Most of its canals remain, and a stroll along the narrow streets offers picture-perfect views.

Tours by Carriage and Boat

Bruges is eminently walkable, but before you start your own exertions take a tour of the streets by horse-drawn carriage or along the small network of canals by boat. If you have the time, try both, as they offer contrasting experiences in different parts of town.

View from Rozenhoedkaai, in Bruges, across to the Belfry

A ride around Bruges

The Markt

Bruges' two town squares are linked by a short street (Breidelstraat). The **Markt** is the larger of the two, and the commercial centre of the town. In the middle of the square stands a 19th-century sculpture, a tribute to Jan Breydel and Pieter de Coninck, the leaders of a 1302 revolt against French overlords. On the southeast side of the square is the **Belfort-Hallen** (Belfry and Covered Market; open daily 9.30am–5pm; Covered Market free; admission fee for Belfry), built in the 13th century. The Belfry was built at the same time, but later extended, and the clock was added in the 15th century. Climb to the top, 366 steps and 84m (276ft) up, for a panoramic view. Part of the way up around the steep stairwell, you pass the 47-bell carillon. Inside the Belfry was the town treasury, and such were the riches of the town that they could only be accessed with nine separate keys. The Markt was once served by a canal that brought goods directly to the market hall. The adjacent 19th-century **Provinciaal Hof** (Provincial Palace) is the seat of the West Flanders provincial government.

The Burg and Town Hall

The **Burg** is the smaller of the two squares, and the oldest, dating to medieval times. It was named after the original castle of Bruges (no longer standing). Each building on the Burg reveals its own beauty, and together, they make one of the most coherent, sequential architectural statements in Europe.

On the south side of the square is the **Stadhuis** (Town Hall; open daily 9.30am–5pm; admission fee), a Gothic master-piece built from 1376 to 1420. Its ornate façade has a wealth of fascinating detail, adorned with statues of the counts of Flanders, family crests and scenes of daily life. Inside, there is even more evidence of civic pride, with guild pennants hanging from the ceiling. The Gothic Hall on the second floor has a magnificent vaulted wooden ceiling decorated with gilt.

To the right of the Stadhuis is the **Landhuis van het Brugse Vrije** (the Palace of the Liberty of Bruges). The mansion is an interesting amalgam of architectural styles. It is renowned for its ornate chimneypiece of marble, alabaster and oak, dating from 1531, in the **Renaissancezaal van het Brugse Vrije** (Renaissance Hall of the Liberty of Bruges; open daily 9.30am–12.30pm and 1.30–5pm, also Easter Mon, Pentecost Mon; admission fee). At its centre is a statue of Emperor Charles V, surrounded by other members of the Habsburg dynasty. At the rear of the complex are the remains of a 16th-century structure that housed the Law Courts. The façade in front of the square is 18th century. Between the Stadhuis and the Landhuis van het Brugse Vrije is the **Oude Civiele Griffie** (Old Recorder's House), completed in 1537.

The Belfry is the signature landmark of Bruges

Inside the Heilig-Bloedbasiliek
(Basilica of the Holy Blood)

Basilica of the Holy Blood

West of the Stadhuis is the entrance to the city's most important religious building. This is the **Heilig-Bloed-basiliek** (Basilica of the Holy Blood; open Apr–Sept daily 9.30–11.50am and 2–5.50pm; Oct–Mar Thur–Tues 10am–noon and 2–3.50pm, Wed 10–11.50am; church free; admission fee to treasury), whose façade was completed in 1534.

Inside, there are two small and richly decorated chapels. The lower chapel is 12th-century Romanesque, while the upper one is 16th-century Gothic in style, with 19th-century alterations. It is in a side room of this upper chapel that the relic that gives the basilica its name is kept. When the Flemish knight Dirk of Alsace returned in 1150 from the Second Crusade, he is said to have brought back a phial containing a fragment of cloth stained with a drop of Christ's blood. The blood was said to have turned liquid on several occasions, and this was declared miraculous by Pope Clement V, and Bruges became a centre of pilgrimage.

In 1611, the archdukes of Spain presented the church with an ornate silver tabernacle in which the phial is now stored. In the early days, the phial was displayed publicly on a weekly basis. Today, it only leaves the side chapel once per year on Ascension Day in May, when it is carried through the streets of Bruges in the Procession of the Holy Blood, one of the most elaborate processions in Belgium. The gold-and-silver reliquary used to transport the phial can be seen in a small treasury just off the chapel.

Opposite the Stadhuis, near the basilica, is the **Proosdij**, formerly the palace of the bishops of Bruges.

Groenerei and Huidenvettersplein
Take the route through the narrow archway between the Stadhuis and the Oude Civiele Griffie. You'll cross one of Bruges' network of canals to **Groenerei** (Green Canal) and see the covered **Vismarkt** (fish market) just ahead. A short walk to the left takes you to the **Pelikaanhuis** (Pelican House), easily identified by the emblem of the bird above the door. Built in 1634 at the point where the canal curves to the right, this was one of many almshouses in the city. There are several boarding points for water trips along the canal-side here, though you may have to queue.

At the diminutive square of **Huidenvettersplein**, several houses are huddled at the water's edge, with a view of the Belfry rising behind and weeping willows softening the red brick. When the tour boats pass on the canal, you can hardly fail to be enchanted.

Fish market motif

Museum of Fine Arts
The street of Dijver runs alongside Groenerei. Here you will find a number of major museums. First is the **Groeninge Museum**, the city's museum of fine arts (open Tues–Sun 9.30am–5pm, also Easter Mon, Pen-

tecost Mon; admission fee), which displays a fine collection of Flemish masters including the work of Jan van Eyck, particularly his *Madonna with Canon George Van der Paele*, of Hieronymus Bosch and Gerard David. Works of later Belgian artists such as René Magritte are also on display. Take a walk around the gardens. The whole vista is typically Flemish, with its low-rise, cottage-style white buildings with red tile roofs.

In the Arentshuis nearby is the **Brangwyn Museum** (open Tues–Sun 9.30am–5pm, also Easter Mon, Pentecost Mon; admission fee), featuring the extensive collection of British Arts and Crafts exponent Sir Frank Brangwyn, who was born in Bruges and bequeathed his work and collection to the city when he died in 1956. As a student of William Morris, Brangwyn is an important link to later artistic movements, and his work is a contrast to the earlier Flemish masters that are so abundant across the city.

Flemish Masters

A group of early Flemish artists, based mostly in Bruges and Ghent, have had their work handed down to us under the banner of the 'Flemish Primitives'. Yet the luminous, revolutionary work of Jan van Eyck (1385–1441), whose *Adoration of the Mystic Lamb* is in Ghent's St Bavo's Cathedral, can scarcely be thought of as primitive. Nor can that of his contemporaries Rogier van der Weyden (c.1399–1464), Hans Memling (c.1430–94) and Petrus Christus (c.1410–72), who shared Van Eyck's fondness for realistic portrayals of human and natural subjects.

Later, the focus of attention switched to Antwerp and, to a lesser degree, to Brussels. The occasionally gruesome works of Pieter Bruegel the Elder (1525–69), the sensuous paintings of Peter Paul Rubens (1577–1640) and the output of Rubens' students Jacob Jordaens (1593–1678) and Antoon van Dyck (1599–1641) cemented the Flemish connection with the finest art of its day.

The **Gruuthuse Museum** (open Tues–Sun 9.30am–5pm, also Easter Mon, Pentecost Mon; admission fee), so called because the original owners of the Gruuthuse Mansion had the right to tax '*gruut*', the basic mash of herbs and spices used in the brewing process, is next.

Four Horsemen of the Apocalypse by Rik Poot

The building housing the museum is itself worth seeing. Erected in the 15th century, it has twice housed fugitive English kings – Henry IV in 1471, and Charles II in 1656. In the garden, a romantic brick bridge crosses one of Bruges' narrower canals, offering yet another picture opportunity. You will also find Rik Poot's modern sculpture, *Four Horsemen of the Apocalypse*, gracing the outer courtyard.

The rooms of the mansion display a wealth of daily articles including furniture and utensils. The huge kitchen is particularly interesting – it looks as if the 15th-century cook has just stepped out of it to do the daily shopping.

At the end of Dijver is the **Onze-Lieve-Vrouwekerk** (Church of Our Lady; open Mon–Fri 9am–12.30pm and 1.30–5pm, Sat 9am–12.30pm and 1.30–4pm, Sun 2–5pm; church free; admission fee to sanctuary of Charles and Mary and museum), an imposing church that has a 122-m (400-ft) brick tower – the second highest in Belgium, after Antwerp Cathedral's. Inside the church you will find the gilded tombs of Charles the Bold and his daughter Mary of Burgundy, whose premature death at the age of 25 brought the Burgundian period of Belgian history to an end. The Church of Our Lady also displays a sculpture of the

The tomb of Mary of Burgundy in the Church of Our Lady

Madonna and Child by Michelangelo, the only one to be exported from Italy during the artist's lifetime.

Hans Memling Museum

Situated opposite the entrance to the church, through an archway, is **Sint-Jans-hospitaal** (St John's Hospital). Dating from the 12th century, it is the oldest building in Bruges. It remained in use until the 19th century. In the old hospital church you will find **Memling in Sint-Jan** (open Tues–Sun 9.30am–5pm, also Easter Mon, Pentecost Mon; admission fee), which is devoted to the work of the German-born master Hans Memling, who settled in Bruges. Although the collection is not extensive, each piece is a particularly fine example. Look for the *Mystic Marriage of St Ursula*; the exquisite detail of this painting makes it one of Belgium's national treasures. The hospital complex also has a pleasant bar/ brasserie with a sun terrace, making it an ideal place to take a break.

Walk south down Mariastraat, with its selection of chocolate and lace shops. A left turn at Wijngardstraat leads to the Begijnhof, but before this, look for the small square of Walplein and **De Halve Maan Brewery** (open for guided tours Apr–Sept daily 11am–4pm; Oct–Dec and Feb–Mar daily 11am–3pm; Jan Sat–Sun 11am–3pm; <www.halvemaan.be>; admission fee), which has been in operation in the city since 1546. A tour of the present brewery, opened in 1856, takes around 45 minutes, and ends with a taste of Bruges' own Straffe Hendrik beer.

The Begijnhof

The **Begijnhof** at Bruges was founded in 1245 by Margaret of Constantinople and was active in providing security for lost and abandoned women until the 20th century. The circular collection of white painted buildings dating from the 17th century – an oasis of solitude even in quiet Bruges – is now home to a community of the Benedictine order. Please respect their request for peace and quiet as you walk through the gardens. Just before the main entrance is an open area with a pretty canal and a range of restaurants. The horse-drawn carriages turn around here on their tours. You'll find a water fountain here for them, decorated with a horse's head.

From the fountain, it is only a couple of minutes walk to the **Minnewater** (Lake of Love) and a picturesque park. Minnewater was originally the inner harbour of Bruges, before the outlet to the sea silted up. Today, you can see the 15th-century gunpowder house and scant remains of a protective wall. You'll find people cycling and jogging along the path here. The open water is a haven for birds, including swans.

The Old Quaysides

The main canal that served the centre of the old town entered from the north.

St John's Hospital, the oldest building in Bruges

Bear at the Burghers' Lodge

Today this terminates at **Jan van Eyckplein**, with a statue of the artist, just a couple of minutes away from the Markt. In the square, you can still find fine buildings lining what were once the busy quaysides of Speigelrei and Spinolarei. The 15th-century **Oud Tolhuis** (Old Toll House) is where taxes on goods entering and leaving the city were collected. Today it is home to the West Flanders Provincial Archives. Nearby is the **Poorters Loge** (Burghers' Lodge), a kind of gentlemen's club for the wealthy businessmen of Bruges' golden age.

Located in Peperstraat, east of the central canal, is the **Kantcentrum** (Lace Centre; open Mon–Fri 10am–noon and 2–6pm, Sat 10am–noon and 2–5pm; <www.kantcentrum. be>; admission fee), a museum and workshop in the 15th-century Jeruzalemgodshuizen (Jerusalem Almshouses). Fine examples of the craft of lace-making, and demonstrations by lacemakers, can be seen.

Ghent

In the 12th century, Ghent (Gent in Dutch and Gand in French) was one of the largest cities in Europe, thriving on its trade in textiles and its position at the confluence of the Leie and Scheldt rivers. Its people were independent and self-assertive; the pagan population threw Christian clergymen into the River Scheldt in 610, and in 1337 they rose up against French rule. Today, it is thriving as a modern commercial town. Thanks to its university, it has a young population, which gives it a vibrancy not felt in Bruges. Ghent also has some interesting historic attractions to enjoy, many of which have undergone extensive restoration in recent times. Much of the town centre is traffic-free, except for the tram services, which adds to the enjoyment of walking. Perhaps the best place to start your tour is at **Sint-Michielsbrug** (St Michael's Bridge), spanning the River Leie just west of the old town. To the left are the old quaysides of Graslei and Korenlei, and beyond them is the medieval castle of Gravensteen. Three of Ghent's landmarks – Sint-Niklaaskerk, Belfort and Sint-Baafskathedraal – lie ahead.

The Church of St Nicholas

The church of **Sint-Niklaas** (St Nicholas) was built from the 13th to the 18th centuries and is therefore an amalgam

Spires of Ghent from Sint-Michielsbrug (St Michael's Bridge)

of architectural styles. Beyond the church is the **Belfort** (Belfry; open daily mid-Mar–mid-Nov 10am–6pm; May–Oct free guided tour daily 2.10, 3.10 and 4.10pm; admission fee), completed in 1380. A recent refurbishment has seen the re-gilding of the clock-face and the dragon that sits atop the spire. You can take a lift to the viewing platform 91m (298ft) above the town, for tremendous views. Housed in the Belfry's Raadskelder (Council Cellar) is the city's tourist information office, the Infokantoor.

Around the Belfry is the **Lakenhalle** (Cloth Hall), a symbol of corporate power when it was completed in 1441. Both the Belfort and Lakenhalle are on Emile Braun-

Ghent's Sint-Baafskathedraal

plein, adjacent to Botermarkt (Butter Market), one of the major meeting places in centuries gone by. In the 16th century, it was decided to build the new **Stadhuis** (Town Hall; guided tours only, reserved in advance at Infokantoor in the Belfry; admission fee) on the north side of the square. Like Sint-Niklaaskerk, the Stadhuis took many decades to complete. Work was halted in 1639 and only recommenced as the 18th century dawned. By this time, of course, a new architectural style was in vogue. You will notice that the building has one Renaissance façade facing Botermarkt, a Baroque one opposite Hoogpoort and a Rococo façade on the Poeljemarkt side.

In summer there are guided tours of the ornate interior; they include the magnificent **Pacificatiezaal** (Pacification Room), where the Pacification of Ghent, a treaty aimed (fruitlessly) at ending the religious wars in the Low Countries, was signed in 1576.

Ghent Altarpiece by Jan van Eyck

St Bavo's Cathedral

The third spire to be seen from Sint-Michielsbrug belongs to **Sint-Baafskathedraal** (St Bavo's Cathedral; open Apr–Oct daily 8.30am–6pm; Nov–Mar daily 8.30am–5pm; cathedral free; admission fee to crypt and *Mystic Lamb* chapel). This imposing granite-and-brick building is also a mixture of architectural styles, with a chancel dating from the 14th century, a nave from the 15th century and a transept from the 16th century.

The art inside the cathedral represents some of Belgium's greatest cultural treasures. To the left of the main entrance is a small chapel containing what has become known as the *Ghent Altarpiece*, a Jan van Eyck masterpiece called *The Adoration of the Mystic Lamb* (1432). Here, Van Eyck achieved reality through painstaking attention to every detail, breaking away from the medieval stylised form. Other masterpieces include *The Conversion of St Bavo* by Rubens and a work by Frans Pourbus, *Christ Amongst the Doctors*, which has many luminaries of the time painted as onlookers in the crowd.

Korenlei and Graslei

Just to the left of Sint-Michielsbrug, **Korenlei** and **Graslei** once formed the main harbour of Ghent, known as Tussen Bruggen (Between the Bridges). Here you can find some of Ghent's finest old buildings, guild houses and warehouses. Both sides of the river are equally beautiful, but on Graslei, look out particularly for the **Gildenhuis van de Vrije Schippers** (House of the Free Boatmen), built in 1531, and Het Spijker (1200), which has been tastefully developed into a bar and eatery. Korenlei rivals its neighbour with the **Gildenhuis van de Onvrije Schippers** (House of the Tied Boatmen), a Flemish Baroque masterpiece dating from 1739, and De Zwane, a former brewery of the 16th century.

Gravensteen

Walk north along the river, and as it splits, you will see the dank grey walls of the **Gravensteen** (open Apr–Sept daily 9am–6pm; Oct–Mar daily 9am–5pm; admission fee) ahead. The outline that Gravensteen presents is the stuff of fairytales (or nightmares): crenellations and turrets, tiny slits for archers to fire their arrows, and a moat to stop invaders. The castle was the seat of the counts of Flanders and from its construction in 1180 it represented their huge power and wealth. Inside you can visit their living quarters, the torture chamber and dungeons, where grisly instruments are on view.

Just to the west of the Leie, the **Design Museum Gent** (open Tues–Sun 10am–6pm; <http://design.museum.gent.be>; admission fee) occupies a 1755 mansion with a central courtyard. The rooms display interior design and furnishings up to the 19th century. A separate wing contains modern furniture.

Patershol

Situated behind the Gravensteen, the **Patershol** district is a jumble of narrow medieval streets, dotted with restaurants and cafés. A short walk leads to the city's folklore museum, **Het Huis van Alijn** (Alijn House; open Tues–Sun 11am–5pm; <www.huisvan alijn.be>; admission fee), housed in a series of restored almshouses that date from 1363. This museum's collection includes numerous everyday articles used in such activities as spinning and weaving, animal husbandry and cooking.

Across the canal, **Vrijdagmarkt** still holds its Friday market, but visitors arrive to view Dulle Griet or Mad Meg at other times of the week. This huge, 16-ton cannon stands on the nearby quayside. There are numerous imposing buildings on Vrijdagmarkt. One of the most prominent is Ons Huis, which dates from 1900.

Colourful façades along Ghent's attractive Korenlei

Citadelpark

Art lovers should not miss the recently refurbished **Museum voor Schone Kunsten** (Museum of Fine Arts; open Tues–Sun 10am–6pm; <www.mskgent.be>; admission fee) in Citadelpark. Artists include Frans Hals, Pieter Breugel the Younger, Rubens and Bosch. The **Stedelijk Museum voor Actuele Kunst** (SMAK; Museum of Modern Art; open Tues–Sun 10am–6pm; <www.smak.be>; admission fee) opposite offers a collection of different 20th-century Belgian artists.

WHAT TO DO

In addition to hundreds of things to see, Brussels also has lots to do, with several important performance venues, a plethora of bars and some delightful shopping opportunities.

SHOPPING

Though there are no 'zones' as such, certain districts do have a greater density of certain speciality shops. The streets around the Grand-Place are filled with shops selling cheap knick-knacks, T-shirts, mugs and keyrings – all the usual budget remembrances but also handmade lace, pralines and crystal. For antiques, head towards the Sablon area, where there are also some excellent art galleries. The weekend antiques market in place du Grand-Sablon is noted for quality items, if not for bargain prices. For bric a brac, head to the flea market at place du Jeu-de-Balle in the Marolles – a veritable treasure trove of memorabilia, furniture, porcelain and glassware. For secondhand and rare books, try Galerie Bortier, uphill from the Grand-Place, whose stores have a huge collection.

For haute couture, visit avenue Louise, the nearby Porte de Namur and the several galleries in between, where fine boutiques and department stores are full of the best European and Belgian fashions. For a selection of high fashion in the centre of town, visit the **Galeries Royales St-Hubert**, built in the 1840s, where Delvaux has its signature store. For modern fashions, try rue Antoine Dansaert, across from the Bourse. Further out, boulevard de Waterloo has numerous good stores along its length.

Left: Galeries Royales St-Hubert

High-street fashion and all the best-known European names can be found on rue Neuve, north of place de la Monnaie. If it's raining, make for the nearby modern shopping malls of Centre Anspach and Centre de la Monnaie. Stamps and coins can be found in numerous shops in the narrow streets around rue du Midi, a few blocks south of the Grand-Place.

Making lace

What to Buy

With a tradition of trade guilds going back to the Middle Ages, it should not be surprising that Brussels still excels in many crafts. Artistic inspiration takes a number of forms, and as you walk along the city streets, there is sure to be something to catch your eye.

Lace. The women in Brussels' *béguinages* and its ladies of the court spent many hours creating fine lace, which adorned clothing and ceremonial garments. Nowadays, this lace is used to decorate handkerchiefs, napkins, table linens and special items such as christening gowns. Prices vary greatly between machine-produced lace and hand-worked items; knowledgeable sales assistants will help by explaining the different qualities of the pieces on display.

Tapestry. Belgium was renowned for its tapestry-making during the reigns of the Burgundians and the Habsburgs. The huge tapestries designed for the ruling families incorporated gold and silver thread and were considered so valuable that they were classed as part of the royal treasury. Today, the tradition continues, but, as with lace, much of the tapestry on sale is machine-produced. Handmade work is exquisite, but comes at a high price. You can buy traditional items such as wall coverings or more modern items such as luggage, clothing, or soft home furnishings (cushions and curtains).

Books and Antiques. For many years Brussels sat on a major trading route, and it is clear from the range of items available in antique and antiquarian bookshops that goods found their way to Belgium from all across Europe, and later, the colonies. Furniture from England and France sits alongside glass from the Habsburg Empire of Eastern Europe. Prices are steep, but the level of expertise in stores around place du Grand-Sablon is equally high.

Silver and Jewellery. Jewellers to the royal court produced beautiful pieces, and today's gold- and silversmiths continue in the same fashion.

Art. Commercial galleries feature the work of established artists and newcomers in a range of genres. Pop art is particularly popular at present, but it is by no means monopolising the arena. You can also buy original cartoon fiches

Lace Society

Belgium has a tradition of making lace – a threadwork of silk, linen or cotton – that stretches back to the 16th century in Flanders. Brussels and Bruges are the principal sales points. Beware of cheap machine-made and imported imitations, unless you want only a simple souvenir. Belgian handmade lace is expensive, but if you like lace this is the only sort worth buying. It should always be purchased from a reputable shop and clearly labelled as having been handmade in Belgium.

from heroes of the celluloid screen, such as Hergé's *Tintin*. A good starting point is the Belgian Comic Strip Centre in rue des Sables *(see page 39)*, but there's also the Tintin Shop at rue de la Colline 13.

Stamps and Coins. A collection of the world's stamps and coins can be found in small dusty shops around the city. There may be something for your collection here, or you can sell or swap your stamps.

Delvaux Handbags. These have been at the height of Belgian fashion for many years. Their simple lines and excellent construction have made them very popular among well-heeled, stylish women in Europe.

Edibles. The delightful chocolate and pralines produced in Belgium are available all across town in presentation boxes for you to take home. Dandoy has been producing *speculoos* biscuits for several generations; you'll find their main shop on rue

Hats off to Belgium's stallholders

au Beurre, just off the Grand-Place. Alternatively, try Marcolini, on rue des Minimes, in the Sablon district, for hand-produced chocolates. Beer is, of course, another option. With hundreds of different types to choose from, you'll need to do some thorough research before making your choice. Many beer retailers have selections ready for you to take home.

Rich and delicious Belgian chocolates galore

ENTERTAINMENT

With more than 30 venues for the performing arts in the city, there will likely be a wealth of performances taking place, by both local and visiting companies, whatever time of year you visit. The galleries of Brussels host a huge number of temporary exhibitions of art from around the world. All the arts are represented, including many new art forms such as video and internet art. Brussels International tourist office in the Grand-Place produces a seasonal pamphlet with details of exhibitions that are taking place while you are in the city.

Theatre and Music

When the museums close at night, Brussels takes on a different character. There are several prominent theatres around the city, including the **Théâtre Royal de la Monnaie** (place de la Monnaie; tel: 02-229 1200), where the seeds of the 'Belgian Revolution' were sown in 1830. It continues to be a major venue, with a programme of opera and ballet. The **Théâtre National de la Communauté Wallonie Bruxelles**

Inside the Théâtre Royal de la Monnaie

(boulevard Emile Jacqmain 111–15; tel: 02-203 4155) produces strong performances. **Théâtre de la Place des Martyrs** (place des Martyrs 22; tel: 02-223 3208), is a converted cinema that is home to the Théâtre en Liberté Company. For a light-hearted view of theatre, try the **Théâtre Royal de Toone** (Impasse Schuddeveld, Petite rue des Bouchers 21; tel: 02-511 7137), a puppet theatre that has been operated by the same family since 1830. They perform classical plays and local folk tales with marionettes.

Classical music venues in Brussels include the glasshouses of **Le Botanique** (rue Royale 236; tel: 02-218 3732) and the **Palais des Beaux-Arts** (rue Ravenstein 23; tel: 02-507 8200), which is now fashionably known as **Bozar**, and which hosts the Queen Elisabeth Music Competition (held on three out of every four years), as well as numerous concerts. The largest venue is **Forest National** south of the city, with an 8,000-seat capacity (avenue du Globe 36; tel: 02-

340 2223). Here, you'll be able to see pop concerts by many international names. For up-and-coming performers, try the **Ancienne Belgique** (boulevard Anspach 110; tel: 02-548 2424); everyone from Edith Piaf to the Clash has played here.

Nightlife

Nightclubs are numerous and popular in Brussels, and each has a different character. Entrance policies can be strict, and if your 'look' doesn't fit you may not be allowed in, so be sure to dress accordingly. Most open around 11pm and don't close until the early morning. Two of the best for visitors are **Le Sud** (rue de l'Ecuyer 43), a café/bar/nightclub frequented by clients of all ages, and **L'Espace de Nuit Capitale** (rue du Marché-aux-Fromages 10), a large club just off the Grand-Place.

For cinemas, there are two main multiplexes that show English-speaking films with French/Dutch subtitles. UGC (place Brouckère; tel: 0900-10440), has eight screens showing the latest Hollywood releases; **Kinepolis** at Bruparck (tel: 0900-00555), is a 26-screen complex with a 600-sq-m IMAX screen. The **Musée du Cinéma** (rue Baron Horta 9; tel: 02-551 1900) screens classic 'talkies' and silent movies every day.

FESTIVALS

Belgium has a number of festivals that have their antecedents in the Middle Ages – a Golden Age for many towns. Brussels holds the **Ommegang** early in July each year. Originally it had a religious significance, but it soon came to celebrate the power of the old trade corporations in the city. Today's festival commemorates the time in 1549 when the guilds and Chambers of Rhetoric, as they were called, paraded their pennants before Emperor Charles V. The Ommegang fell into disuse, but was revived in 1930. Today the modern bearers of

Flower market, Grand-Place

the head of the guilds dress in costumes of the mid-1500s and carry the banners and pennants of their trades around the Grand-Place.

The **Carpet of Flowers** is a biennial celebration held in mid-August in the Grand-Place, when a huge elaborate tapestry of begonias almost fills the square.

Bruges' greatest festivity takes place usually in the latter part of May each year (on Ascension Day, the fifth Thursday after Easter), when the whole town comes out to witness the **Procession of the Holy Blood** (*Heilig-Bloed-processie*). At this time, the most holy relic of the cathedral, said to contain a drop of Christ's blood, is paraded around the city. Solemn religious services are held across the city before the merrymaking begins.

SPORTS

With over 30 sq m (320 sq ft) of green space for each resident of Brussels, and a surrounding landscape without any appreciable hills, it is easy to understand why sports are a big part of the city's life.

Cycling. This is a popular sport, though not in the centre of Brussels, where there are a number of deceptive inclines to watch out for (to say nothing of the dangerous traffic conditions). In the suburbs and through the forests there are cycle routes and some urban areas have cycle lanes. It is easy to rent bikes – many railway stations have a bike hire office. Don't forget to wear a cycling helmet.

Football. This is a passion in Belgium, as in most other European countries. Royal Sporting Club d'Anderlecht is one of the most successful teams, with a respectable international history to its credit. For details, contact the stadium at avenue Théo Verbeeck 2, Anderlecht (tel: 02-522 1539). The season runs from September to May. The National Stadium (Stade Roi Baudouin) is at Heysel. It holds international games, cup finals, and other national sporting events (tel: 02-473 3940).

Horse-Riding. The Bois de la Cambre and Forêt de Soignes have bridleways for horse-riding.

Jogging and Running. Both are popular, and you are sure to see people taking a turn around the parks. The Brussels Marathon takes place in September.

Leisure Centres. Because the weather in Belgium is often inclement, there are many covered sports complexes in Brussels. The Centre Sportif de Woluwe-Saint-Pierre, avenue Salomé 2 (tel: 02-773 1820), has squash, outdoor and indoor tennis, a swimming pool, sauna and Turkish bath.

Walking. The leafy Forêt de Soignes is the perfect place for forgetting the city and surrounding yourself with birdsong. There are marked routes for walkers.

Water Sports. There's rowing and pedalo rides on local lakes. Visit the lakes at Tervuren, Bois de la Cambre and Forêt de Soignes.

Forêt de Soignes

BRUSSELS FOR CHILDREN

At first glance, Brussels may not seem the best place to take children. However, the city reveals some interesting and entertaining things that are bound to keep your children happy. Carriage rides are great fun, allowing children to rise above the sea of heads for a better view. These take place in Brussels, Antwerp and Ghent during the summer, and in Bruges all year round. You can take a canal or river cruise in Antwerp, Bruges and Ghent.

The **Bruparck** complex has several different attractions. **L'Océade** offers water sports, rides and pools – great on a hot summer day. **Mini-Europe** is the 'child-size' attraction, and is both fun and educational. The eruption of Vesuvius is probably the most popular, with its ground-shaking power.

Many of Brussels' museums have fun and educational attractions that are specifically designed with children in mind. **Scientastic** in the Bourse métro station has simple, hands-on experiments and 'magic' tricks, and the **Natural Sciences Museum**, with its dinosaurs to enthrall young imaginations, also has special activities and workshops for children aged 4–12 years. Covering a subject close to many children's hearts – comic strips – is the **Centre Belge de la Bande Dessinée**. The Dynamusée in the **Cinquantenaire Museum** complex offers special activities for children aged 6–12 years, and the **Musical Instruments Museum** offers multi-sensory experimentation with sound, along with training courses and workshops.

There is a **Children's Museum** at rue du Bourgmestre 15 (tel: 02-640 0107) that operates a regular programme of sessions involving painting, collage, woodworking and theatre for young children. The **Théâtre Royal de Toone** puppet theatre in Petite rue des Bouchers has live performances throughout the year. Many activities specifically for children are conducted in French and Dutch. For details of programmes in English, contact each organisation directly.

Castles always spark the imagination and **the Gravensteen** in Ghent is no exception. Images of sword fights on the battlements and prisoners in the dungeons flash through the mind.

The parks and forests provide perfect environments in which to walk, cycle or ride. The lake at **Tervuren** has boats for hire. If you prefer something more relaxing, take a rug and a picnic and just enjoy the sunshine; don't forget to take some bread to feed the ducks and geese.

Open space at the Atomium, a giant model of an iron crystal

If you and your family really need a break from the city's sights and sounds, then try the **Walibi** and **Aqualibi**, situated only 19km (12 miles) southeast of Brussels. The huge Walibi theme park has mechanical rides with spirals, catapults, river rapids and an attraction entitled *1,001 Arabian Nights*. Aqualibi water park has cascades, whirlpools and jungle experiences. There are numerous opportunities for refreshment, so you can spend the whole day here. (To reach the theme park by car, take the E411 and leave at the Brussels Namur exit; by train, take the Ottignies/Louvain-la-Neuve line, get off at Bierges station, which is only 300m (330yds) from the park entrance.)

Calendar of Events

Brussels holds numerous annual events throughout the year. Many of these happen around the same time every year, but exact dates are subject to change, so check with Brussels International tourist office *(see page 128)* before planning a trip around one of these events.

February Mardi Gras, carnival parades in several communes.

April Baroque Spring in the Sablon, classical music performances. The Queen Elisabeth International Music Competition (held on three out of four years).

April–May Royal Greenhouses *(Serres)* at Laeken open to the public.

April–October Festival of Flanders, classical music events in abbeys, cathedrals and city halls throughout Flanders.

May KunstenFESTIVALdesArts: two weeks of dance, theatre and opera performances at venues throughout the city. Museums day: on one day in May many Brussels museums offer free entrance.

Late May Procession of the Holy Blood in Bruges. Brussels Jazz Marathon, an international jazz festival with venues around the city.

June Brussels open-air music festival in the city's squares and parks.

June–August A daily sound-and-light show in the Grand-Place.

June–October Festival of Wallonia, classical music performances are staged in Wallonia.

July Ommegang procession on the first Tuesday and Thursday of the month. Belgium's National Day, 21 July: fireworks at place des Palais. Ghent Festivities, a medieval fair and street entertainment.

July–September The Palais Royal is open to the public.

August Canal Festival, Bruges – every three years (next 2008, 2011…).

9 August Planting of the Maypole.

15 August Carpet of Flowers: Every even-numbered year on this day, a flower carpet is laid out on the Grand-Place.

September Brussels Marathon. Antwerp's Feast of Liberation and Festival of the Guilds.

December Unveiling of Christmas crib and lights in the Grand-Place, and Christmas market and ice-skating rink at the Marché aux Poissons.

EATING OUT

Brussels has no shortage of fine restaurants, and its people enjoy eating out. Belgium does not have to look abroad for good food. It has a fine national and regional cuisine of its own, with hearty dishes based on fresh local ingredients. In addition, chefs have added personal twists to the national dishes of their neighbours to produce their own unique creations. There are numerous eateries in the city, from formal to informal, with a range of prices, so you should find something to match your taste and budget.

As a cosmopolitan city, Brussels has some excellent international restaurants offering French, Chinese, Vietnamese, Greek, Moroccan and Japanese cuisine, among others. However, if you want to try Belgian cuisine, the information in this chapter will help you through the menu.

Some Brussels restaurants are happy to allow diners' dogs into the dining room, and many let them on to outside terraces. Smoking is not allowed in restaurants, although it is still permitted in cafés and snack-bars.

WHEN TO EAT

French fries make a great snack

Eating in Brussels means fitting your appetite into set hours. Few restaurants stay open throughout the day. Lunch *(déjeuner)* is between noon and 2.30pm, while dinner *(diner)* is usually from 6pm until 10.30 or 11pm.

However, don't worry that you won't be able to

eat at all in the afternoon in Brussels. There are numerous informal *brasseries* and cafés that serve food – though perhaps with a simpler menu – throughout the day. Look out for signs saying 'nonstop' outside an establishment, which simply means what it says.

WHAT TO EAT

There is a wide variety of speciality Belgian dishes, both Flemish and Walloon. Many local dishes are seasonal, so depending on what time of year you travel, you might not see all those mentioned below on the menu. The best restaurants serving Belgian food will change their menus several times each year to take seasonal offerings into account.

Among hors d'œuvres, there is a beer soup *(soupe à la bière)* with chicken stock and onions; a cold pâté of veal, pork and rabbit known as *potjesvlees*; *flamiche*, a savoury cheese pie with leeks or onions; *tomate aux crevettes*, tomato filled with shrimp and mayonnaise; and *croquettes de crevette*, small patties of shrimp. Fine smoked ham *(jambon d'Ardenne)* from the forests to the east is also served, thinly sliced with pickles.

Main Dishes

Belgium specialises in stews. The slow-cooked meat is always tender, the sauce tasty and the vegetables never overcooked. The only 'difficulty' lies in the portions, particularly at the smaller local brasseries, where they tend to be huge.

The best-known main dish is probably *waterzooï*, chicken (or sometimes fish) stewed with whites of leeks, potatoes, bouillon, cream and egg yolks. *Anguille au vert* is eel flavoured with green herbs, usually sorrel, sage and parsley. *Carbonnades flamandes* is a dish consisting of lean beef browned in a pan and then cooked in a casserole with lots of onions and beer. *Pavé des brasseurs* is a chateaubriand steak with beer sauce. Oxtail *(queue de boeuf)* is served in a savoury *gueuze* beer sauce *(see box, page 103)*. Hochepot, a pot-au-feu based on oxtail or pigs' feet, ears and snouts, is another Flemish stew. *Lapin à la flamande* is rabbit marinated in beer and vinegar and braised in onions and prunes. High-quality game usually comes from the Ardennes region to the east, including hare *(lièvre)*, venison *(chevreuil)* and pheasant *(faisan)*. If you like ham, try *jamboneau*, a shank of ham cooked with cream and served with potatoes and vegetables. *Boudin rouge* or *noir* is blood sausage, while *boudin blanc* is a lighter version of the same, enlivened by aromatic herbs; all are popular dishes, served with potato purée and an apple compôte.

Al fresco on the Grand-Place

Vegetables

The Belgian countryside produces top-quality vegetables, and these not only make excellent accompaniments to meat and fish, but also form popular main courses in their own right.

Vegetable dishes include *chou rouge à la flamande*, or red cabbage cooked with apples, onions, red wine and vinegar; and *chicon* (braised endives), often served *gratiné au four* (baked with cheese and ham). During the months of April and May, you can find rare delicacies of hop flowers *(jets de houblon)* served with poached eggs and *mousseline* sauce. In spring try *asperges de Malines*, local white asparagus dressed with melted butter and crumbled hard-boiled egg, and *choux de Bruxelles* (Brussels sprouts), often prepared with chestnuts and pieces of bacon, and cooked in goose fat.

Seafood

Even the east of Belgium is only a couple of hours from the sea, so seafood plays a large part in the national cuisine. Most Belgian towns have a fish market that has been in operation for many centuries, and Brussels has long been a big market for retailers and restaurateurs.

Moules (mussels) are probably the most famous Belgian dish. Harvested mostly from nearby Zeeland province in Holland, they are delivered fresh to the capital each morning. Served steaming in a huge bowl, they come with a variety of sauces – *marinières* (white wine and cream), *moutarde* (mustard) and more besides.

One option to try is an assortment of fresh seafood, known as an *assiette de fruits de mer* (seafood platter). These dishes may include anything from mussels *(moules)* and spiny lobster *(langoustines)* to oysters *(huîtres)*, crabs *(crabes)*, whelks *(boulots)*, shrimps *(crevettes)* and sea urchins *(oursins)*. Along rue des Bouchers you can watch your plate take shape as a selection is chosen from the display of seafood on ice nearby. Or you could try a fillet or whole fish, delicately

Fish at the market

cooked to preserve its fresh-
ness. Try salmon *(saumon)*,
sole *(sole)*, bream *(daurade)*,
mullet *(rouget)* or sea bass
(loup de mer).

Desserts

Most restaurants offer
cheese as a dessert option.
Among as many as 300
different locally produced
cheeses are the very strong
remoudou, the *djotte de
Nivelles* and cream cheeses
from Brussels.

Crêpes (pancakes) are
extremely popular here and
are served with a variety of
accompaniments. Try them
aux pommes (with apples)
or *à la grecque,* with icing

Mussels are a Belgian speciality

sugar and powdered spices. Or look out for the two-layered
pancake with a tasty cheese filling, known as a *double*.
Other desserts include *beignets de Bruxelles* (doughnuts or
fritters), *tarte au riz* (rice tart), *manons* (chocolates filled
with fresh cream) and the famous *speculoos* (spicy ginger-
bread biscuits cut into shapes). Strawberries and other fresh
fruit usually appear on restaurant menus all year round, but
are best in summer when they are ripened naturally.

For those whose sweet tooth has not been satisfied yet,
try fine pralines, local chocolates with delicate fillings of
great subtlety both in flavour and variety. Chocolate
gateaux take on a spectacular transformation from the
ordinary to the divine at the hands of Belgian *chocolatiers*.

Belgian chocolates and pralines are exported all over the world, but the best can still be found in Brussels.

Snacks

Waffles *(gaufres)* are the best-known dessert of Belgian origin and these are usually eaten in the street smothered with syrup, or at cafés with a generous helping of chocolate syrup or whipped cream.

If you're looking for a savoury snack to tide you over until the next meal, then try the famous *frites* (French fries), available day and night at special stands *(friteries,* or, in Flemish, *frietekotten)* and usually served in paper cones with salt and mayonnaise. *Caricoles* (sea snails) are another street speciality. Eat them piping hot with the spicy broth in which they were cooked. You will also find a full range of sandwiches on offer. The most popular local bread for sandwiches is the *pistolet,* a small, crusty round roll.

Drinks

Coffee – hot, dark and strong – is the local drink of choice by day. If you want it with milk, ask for it *au lait.* Bars always serve coffee, tea and hot chocolate in addition to alcoholic drinks, a full range of international-brand spirits plus soft drinks or sodas. Try the local gin, which is known as *pèkèt.*

The local brew

Most restaurants have a wine list – and some, particularly at the top end of the market, have very good cellars – and will offer you a good-value house wine in addition to more expensive bottles. Brasseries and smaller restaurants also offer house wine in half-litre and litre *pichets* or carafes. These are normally simple, but drinkable wines that pair well with the hearty meals on offer.

Belgian Beer

Belgium is renowned worldwide for its beer. Historically, the cultivation of hops and barley was under the control of the many local monasteries. This resulted in high standards and differing flavours; indeed one particular type of beer, *gueuze*, can only be produced in a small region of the Senne Valley near Brussels because the micro-organisms that give the beer its distinct flavour are only found there.

Beer in Belgium is treated with the same degree of reverence as fine wine in France. There are numerous small breweries scattered around the country, producing small quantities of beer for the local market. Each is served in its own style of glass either from the bottle as you watch or from the tap, known as *pression*. Some have a high alcohol content. If you are unsure about which to choose, here is a short introduction to the range of beers you will find on your bar list.

Blanche. A cloudy blond beer made from wheat. Low in alcohol and very refreshing, it is a good option for a sightseeing break.

Brune. Darker beer.

Lambic. A beer that ferments spontaneously after exposure to the air. Now only produced by smaller independent breweries (a Belgian speciality). Very yeasty in flavour.

Gueuze. A lambic beer that has been allowed to ferment a second time.

Kriek. A lambic beer with the essence of fresh fruit that has been left to develop in huge vats. Cherry is the most popular.

Trappist. This is the strongest beer in Belgium. It is full-flavoured, dark in colour, with a distinctive smell of malt. Trappist beers date from the time of the monasteries and are enjoying a period of renewed popularity today.

To Help You Order…

	French	*Dutch*
Could we have a table?	**Pouvons-nous avoir une table?**	*Heeft u een tafel voor ons?*
Do you have a set menu?	**Avez-vous un menu du jour?**	*Heeft u een menu van de dag?*
I'd like a/an/ some …	**J'aimerais …**	*Ik zou graag hebben …*
beer	**une bière**	*een pils*
butter	**du beurre**	*boter*
bread	**du pain**	*brood*
cheese	**du fromage**	*kaas*
coffee	**un café**	*koffie*
egg(s)	**un (des) œuf(s)**	*een ei (eieren)*
menu	**la carte**	*een menu*
sugar	**du sucre**	*suiker*
tea	**du thé**	*thee*
wine	**du vin**	*wijn*

…and Read the Menu in French

agneau	lamb	**oie**	goose
bœuf	beef	**petits pois**	peas
canard	duck	**pommes**	apples
champignons	mushrooms	**pommes de terre**	potatoes
chou	cabbage		
choufleur	cauliflower	**porc**	pork
crevettes	shrimps	**poulet**	chicken
épinards	spinach	**pruneaux**	prunes
fraises	strawberries	**raisins**	grapes
haricots verts	green beans	**riz**	rice
jambon	ham	**rognons**	kidneys
lapin	rabbit	**saucisse**	sausage
moules	mussels	**veau**	veal

...and in Dutch

aardappelen	potatoes	*konijn*	rabbit
aardbeien	strawberries	*mosselen*	mussels
bloemkool	cauliflower	*nieren*	kidneys
druiven	grapes	*pruimen*	prunes
eend	duck	*rodekool*	red
forel	trout		cabbage
frieten	French	*rund*	beef
(fries)	fries	*spruitjes*	Brussels
garnalen	shrimps		sprouts
haas	hare	*tong*	sole
kaas	cheese	*uien*	onions
kalfskotelet	veal chop	*varkensvlees*	pork
karbonade	chop	*vis*	fish
kip	chicken	*worst*	sausage

Enjoying a beer at a pavement café

HANDY TRAVEL TIPS

An A–Z Summary of Practical Information

A

ACCOMMODATION
(see also YOUTH HOSTELS and BUDGETING FOR YOUR TRIP)

Brussels has a large number of hotels from which to choose – everything from big, luxurious places to small, budget affairs. The Brussels International tourist office publishes a booklet containing information about all hotels in the greater Brussels area, and includes images of each establishment. The tourist offices in the city can make same-day reservations for you if you arrive without a booking. There is also a central reservations service: Resotel, avenue de l'Atlantique 122, 1150 Brussels; tel: 02-779 3939; fax: 02-779 3900; <www.belgiumhospitality.com>. (For more information, *see page 130.*)

AIRPORT *(aéroport/luchthaven)*

Brussels National Airport (tel: 02-753 4221; <www.brusselsairport.be>) is the major international airport for all of Belgium. It lies 14km (9 miles) northeast of the city. There are frequent connections with other European cities and many cities in the US. For information regarding arrivals and departures, tel: 0900-70000 in Belgium; tel: 32-22-753 7753 from outside the country.

The Airport/City Express railway links the airport with the city centre from 5.30am–11.45pm. Departures are every 15 minutes.

Do you have a single/ double room?	**Avez-vous une chambre pour une/deux personnes?** *Hebt u een eenpersoonskamer/ tweepersoonskamer?*
with bath/shower?	**avec bain/douche** *met een bad/douche*
What's the rate per night?	**Quel est le prix pour une nuit?** *Hoeveel kost het per nacht?*

The travelling time is approximately 25 minutes. These trains stop at the city's Gare du Nord, Gare Centrale and Gare du Midi stations, so it's helpful to know which station is nearest to your hotel. Some taxis offer reduced-price return fares – look for a sticker in the corner of the windshield with a white aeroplane on an orange background. Official taxis have blue-and-yellow stickers. Express bus services run from the airport to the centre of Brussels and to Gare du Nord.

Where can I get a taxi?	**Où puis-je trouver un taxi?**
	Waar kan ik een taxi nemen?
How much is it to Brussels city centre?	**Combien coûte la course jusqu'au centre de Bruxelles?**
	Hoeveel kost het naar het centrum van Brussel?
Does this bus go to Brussels?	**Ce bus va-t-il à Bruxelles?**
	Gaat deze bus naar Brussel?

B

BICYCLE HIRE *(location de bicyclette/fietsverhuur)*

Brussels and the surrounding countryside are well equipped for cyclists, with special bike lanes. However, the city itself has a number of deceptive gradients and busy, aggressive traffic. Renting a bike is worthwhile for journeys to the Bois de la Cambre and Fôret de Soignes, or out to Tervuren. Pro Vélo offers bicycle hire and guided cycling tours of the city (rue de Londres 15; tel: 02-502 7355; <www.provelo.org>).

| I'd like to hire a bicycle. | **J'aimerais louer une bicyclette.** | *Ik zou graag een fiets huren.* |

BUDGETING FOR YOUR TRIP

Brussels can be expensive, but no more than any other major European city. Here are a few sample prices to help with your budgeting. Prices are in euros (€).

Getting to Belgium. The cost of getting to Belgium from the UK and Ireland by air varies enormously. Flying with Ryanair one-way from various airports in both countries to Brussels-Charleroi can cost as little as a few pounds or euros (plus taxes), but £10–30 (€15–45) is probably nearer the average. These rates have forced carriers such as BA, BMI, Virgin Express, Aer Lingus and SN Brussels Airlines to cut their own fares.

Of the other options, going by bus from London is likely to be the cheapest. By train, Eurostar from London to Brussels offers good excursion and advance-purchase deals, as does the Channel Tunnel car-transporter. The cost of going by ferry to Zeebrugge or (no foot passengers) Ostend varies depending on the route, whether travelling as a foot passenger or with a car, and whether a cabin is desired. For a foot passenger, the price varies from about £30 one-way on short crossings to about £100 on long crossings.

Similarly, the cost of transatlantic flights from North America varies greatly (particularly given the uncertainties of post-9/11 and bankruptcies among US carriers). A ticket from a consolidator (bucket-shop), or on a special offer, might still be as low as $500 return.

Accommodation. For a double room with bathroom and breakfast, you can pay less than €50, but for reasonable comfort and facilities, €75–100 is a more realistic starting point; a mid-range hotel will cost €100–250; and expensive hotels begin at €250. What you get varies with the location and the time of year. At times when there are major conventions or important European meetings, rooms in the better hotels can be hard to come by.

Eating Out. You can eat well in many Brussels restaurants for less than €25 per person for a three-course meal without wine, but, again, a more reasonable starting point would be around

€40–50; in mid-range establishments, expect to pay €50–75; and in expensive restaurants, above €75.

Car Hire. Expect to pay €60–80 per day for a small car.

Museums. Public museums charge €3–6 for adult admission. Privately owned attractions may cost up to €10. Often, there are reduced rates for children, senior citizens and students. The Brussels Card (24 hours €20; 48 hours €28; 72 hours €33) offers reduced entry prices to many attractions and a public transport pass (see TOURIST INFORMATION).

Public Transport. Tickets for one journey that is interchangeable between buses, trams and metro: €1.50 (€2 when purchased onboard); one-day pass, €4; 10-journey ticket €11 (see PUBLIC TRANSPORT).

C

CAR HIRE *(location de voitures/autoverhuur)*

With a city centre as compact as that in Brussels, and a well-organised public transport system, there is little need for a car. If you wish to explore the countryside, hiring a vehicle for a couple of days frees you from public transport schedules. All the major car-hire firms are represented in the city.

Your national driver's licence will be accepted, provided you have held it for at least a year. Minimum age limits for hiring vary between 20 and 25 years depending on the company and the size of your hire vehicle. Collision Damage Waiver is available, but expensive.

I'd like to rent a car.	**Je voudrais louer une voiture.**
	Ik zou graag een auto huren.
now/tomorrow	**tout de suite/demain**
	nu/morgen
for one day/one week	**pour une journée/une semaine**
	voor een dag/een week

The major international firms all have desks at Brussels National Airport Arrivals Lounge, and offices around the city, and can be contacted for reservations as follows:

Avis: tel: 070-223001; <www.avis.be>.
Budget: tel: 02-753 2170; <www.budget.be>.
Hertz: tel: 02-720 6044; <www.hertz.be>.
Europcar: tel: 02-348 9212; <www.europcar.be>.

CLIMATE

Brussels and the west of Belgium have a temperate maritime climate, which means that they generally have warm, wet summers and cool, wet winters. In summer, there may be as many as seven hours of sunshine per day, with temperatures above 27°C (80°F); however, showers are always a possibility. Winter temperatures drop, but rarely fall below freezing. Rain can be expected just about every day. You can obtain a current weather forecast by telephoning 0900-27003, or going to <www.meteo.be>.

Average daytime temperatures in Brussels:

	J	F	M	A	M	J	J	A	S	O	N	D
°C	5	6	10	13	19	21	23	22	20	14	8	6
°F	41	43	50	55	66	70	74	72	68	57	46	41

CLOTHING

Given the above information about climate, about the only item you will definitely need regardless of the time of year is an umbrella. In summer, the weather can be pleasantly hot, and trousers, T-shirts, shirts and shorts will certainly be useful. However, do not forget to pack a warmer layer, in case there is a cold spell, and a rainproof outer layer. On most evenings you will require a jacket to walk around. In winter, pack warm clothing in addition to a waterproof layer. Don't forget comfortable shoes for sightseeing. Although there are many formally dressed businesspeople, Brussels is a casual city with few dress restrictions. If you intend to visit the theatre, ballet, opera or one of the top restaurants in the city, you should pack something a little more formal, of course. A few restaurants do expect a tie and jacket.

CRIME AND SAFETY (see also EMERGENCIES and POLICE)

Brussels is a relatively safe city by European standards, with little serious threat of major crime against visitors. Petty crime can cause problems, and pickpocketing is a threat, particularly during events that attract large numbers of people (such as the jazz festival).

Serious crime is unlikely to be a worry for visitors to Belgium, but it does exist, and is to an extent a growing problem in some cities, including Brussels and Antwerp. Violent offences are rare, but drugs-related muggings and other crimes are increasing. After dark, stay alert if you are in metro and railway stations, or red-light areas; avoid deserted and poorly lit areas and stay out of city centre parks unless there are plenty of other law-abiding people around.

To minimise the risk of becoming a victim, take a few precautions. Do not carry large amounts of cash or valuables with you. Leave your

Where's the nearest police station?	**Où est le commissariat de police le plus proche?** *War is het dichtsbijzijnde politiebureau?*
I want to report a theft.	**Je veux porter plainte pour vol.** *Ik wil graag een diefstal melden.*
My handbag/wallet/ passport has been stolen.	**On m'a volé mon sac à main/mon portefeuille/mon passeport.** *Mijn handtas/geldbeurs/ paspoort is gestolen.*
Help! Thief!	**A l'aide! Au voleur!** *Hulp! Dief!*

valuables in the hotel safe. Carry all cash and credit cards in secure pockets. Keep handbags shut and carry them close to your body. Do not leave anything in your hire car, if you have one – crime involving vehicles is one of the most common crimes in the city. When walking back to your hotel at night, choose well-lit streets to reach your destination. It's also advisable to park your car in an area that is well lit.

CUSTOMS AND ENTRY REQUIREMENTS

To enter Belgium for stays of up to three months, visitors from European Union (EU) countries need only an identity card, or a passport if your home country has no identity card. Citizens of most other countries, including the US, Canada, Australia, New Zealand and South Africa must be in possession of a valid passport, and in the case of some other countries, of a visa also. Residents of Europe and North America are not subject to health requirements; residents of other countries may be and should check with the local Belgian embassy or consulate before departing for Belgium.

As Belgium belongs to the EU, free exchange of non-duty-free goods for personal use is permitted between Belgium and the UK and Ireland, and other EU countries. There are generous guideline levels of goods for personal use; visitors who bring in or take out greater quantities than these may be required to prove that the excess is for personal use. Residents of non-EU countries may bring in 200 cigarettes or 100 cigarillos or 50 cigars or 250g tobacco; 2 litres still wine; 1 litre spirits or 2 litres sparkling or fortified wine; 50g perfume; 0.25 litres eau de toilette.

I've nothing to declare.	**Je n'ai rien à déclarer.**
	Ik heb niets aan te geven.
It's for my personal use.	**C'est pour mon usage personnel.**
	Het is voor mijn persoonlijk gebruik.

D

DRIVING (see also CAR HIRE)

To take your car into Belgium, you'll need:
• an international driver's licence or your own driver's licence (held for at least one year)
• car-registration papers
• Green Card (this does not provide cover, but is internationally recognised proof that you have insurance; though not obligatory for EU countries, it's still useful, especially in case of an accident)
• a fire extinguisher and a red warning triangle in case of break-down
• a national identity sticker for your car
• for right-hand-drive vehicles, headlight adapters to prevent the lights dazzling other drivers

Driving conditions. Drive on the right, and pass on the left. Although you may wish to drive between towns and cities, it is ill-advised to drive within the big cities themselves. Driving is invariably aggressive, and there are complex one-way systems and intersections to negotiate, along with (in some cities) trams, which you are not allowed to overtake and to which you must give way.

Seat belts must be worn by both driver and passengers. The use of dipped headlights is mandatory after dusk and in poor visibility. There are stiff penalties for driving under the influence of alcohol and drugs, and for speeding. Some offences require payment of fines on the spot, with the offender's car impounded until payment is received.

Drivers should normally give way to traffic approaching from the right. A yellow diamond-shaped sign with a white border indicates that drivers on main roads have right of way; if the sign has a diagonal line through it, drivers must give way to traffic entering from the right.

Motorways. Belgium's motorway *(autoroute/snelweg)* network is excellent, but it and the city ring roads, especially those of Brussels and Antwerp, can get clogged with traffic at peak times. Other main roads are generally relatively free of traffic and weekday travelling is usually smooth. Belgium's accident record, however, is one of the worst in Europe.

Speed limits. On motorways, the limit is 120km/h (75mph); on other main roads it is 90km/h (55mph). In residential areas the speed limit drops to 50km/h (30mph). In all cases, lower limits may be indicated.

Are we on the right road for…?	**Est-ce la bonne route pour…?** *Zijn wij op de juiste weg naar…?*

Parking. There is limited street parking in city centres. Car and coach parks exist in the centres, or in the case of pedestrian-friendly towns such as Bruges, around the perimeter of the centre.

Breakdowns. Belgium's two main motoring organisations are the Touring Club de Belgique and the Royal Automobile Club de Belgique. These have reciprocal arrangements with other national motoring organisations and should be able to help you if you are a member of your own national organisation. In case of breakdown, call Touring Secours/Wegenhulp, tel: 070-344777.

There's been an accident.	**Il y a eu un accident.** *Er is een ongeval gebeurd.*
My car has broken down.	**Ma voiture est en panne.** *Mijn wagen is kapot.*

Fuel and oil: Petrol stations are plentiful, and most international brands of unleaded and diesel fuel are on sale.

Road signs. International pictographs are in widespread use, but here are some written signs you may encounter:

Arrêtez-vous	*Halt*	Halt
Carrefour	*Kruispunt*	Crossroads
Forte pente	*Gevaarlijke Daling*	Steep hill
Déviation	*Omweg*	Detour
Passage piétons	*Voetganger-*	Pedestrian
	oversteekplaats	crossing
Stationnement	*Parkeren*	
autorisé	*Toegelaten*	Parking permitted
Stationnement		
interdit	*Parkeerverbod*	No parking
Prudence	*Voorzichtig Rijden*	Drive with care
Arrêt de bus	*Bushalte*	Bus stop
Stop	*Stop*	Stop
Sens unique	*Eenrichtingsverkeer*	One-way
Danger	*Gevaar*	Danger
Sens interdit	*Verboden Toegang*	No entry
Serrez à droite/	*Rechterhand/*	Keep right/left
à gauche	*Linkerhand Houden*	
Impasse	*Doodlopende Weg*	No through road

E

ELECTRICITY

Belgium operates on 230 (220–240 volts), 50Hz AC, requiring standard two-pin round continental plugs. Visitors should bring – or buy locally – their own adapters, and transformers if needed.

EMBASSIES, CONSULATES AND HIGH COMMISSIONS
(ambassades; consulats/ambassades; consulaten)

Australia: rue Guimard 6–8, 1040 Brussels, tel: 02-286 0500.
Canada: avenue de Tervuren 2, 1040 Brussels, tel: 02-741 0611.
Ireland: rue Wiertz 50, 1040 Brussels, tel: 02-235 6676.
New Zealand: square de Meeûs 1, 1000 Brussels, tel: 02-512 1040.
South Africa: rue de la Loi 26, 1040 Brussels, tel: 02-285 4400.
UK: rue d'Arlon 85, 1000 Brussels, tel: 02-287 6211.
US: boulevard du Régent 25–7, 1000 Brussels, tel: 02-508 2111.

EMERGENCIES (see also CRIME AND SAFETY and POLICE)

Police	**101**
Ambulance	**100**
Fire	**100**

G

GAY AND LESBIAN TRAVELLERS

For information on Brussels and Wallonia, contact the gay and lesbian community centre, **Tels Quels**, rue du Marché-au-Charbon 81, Brussels, tel: 02-502 0070; <www.telsquels.be>. In Flanders, contact the **Federatie Werkgroepen Homoseksualiteit**, Kamnesstraat 22, Ghent, tel: 09-238 2626; <www.holebifoon.be>. The age of consent for gay men is 16.

GETTING THERE

By Air. Many airlines offer direct scheduled flights to Brussels National Airport *(see page 107)*. Brussels Airlines (tel: 070-351111; <www.brusselsairlines.com>) is the main local carrier. British Airways (tel: 0870-850 9850 in the UK; in Belgium, tel: 02-717 3217; <www.ba.com>) operates flights from several UK airports to Brussels. Flight time from London to Brussels is about one hour. Several other airlines operate flights from UK airports to Brussels. They include BMI (tel:

0870-607 0555 in the UK; in Belgium, tel: 02-713 1284; <www.
flybmi.com>) and KLM (tel: 0870-507 4074 in the UK; in Belgium, tel:
070-225335; <www.klm.com>). Aer Lingus (tel: 0818-365000 in Ireland; in Belgium, tel: 070-359901; <www.aerlingus.com>) has regular service to Brussels from Dublin and other Irish airports. Ryanair
(tel: 0871-246 0000 in the UK; in Ireland, tel: 0818-303030; in Belgium, tel: 0902-88007; <www.ryanair.com>) flies from airports in
Britain and Ireland to Charleroi, near Brussels.

American Airlines (tel: 800-433 7300 in the US; in Belgium, tel: 02-
711 9799; <www.aa.com>), Delta Airlines (tel: 800-221 1212 in the
US; in Belgium, tel: 02-711 9799; <www.delta.com>), United Airlines
(tel: 800-538 2929 in the US; in Belgium, tel: 02-713 3600; <www.
united.com>); and Continental Airlines (tel: 800-525 0280 in the US;
in Belgium, tel: 02-643 3939; <www.continental.com>) offer flights
to Brussels. From Canada, Air Canada (tel: 888-247 2262 in Canada;
in Belgium, tel: 070-220100; <www.aircanada.ca>) flies to Brussels.

By Rail. Thalys is a high-speed rail network run by a co-operation of
Belgian, Dutch, German and French companies. It operates frequent
departures from various northern European cities. For information
and reservations in Belgium, tel: 02-528 2828; <www.thalys.com>.

Eurostar operates train services from London through the Channel Tunnel to Brussels. There are frequent departures and the journey time is just over three hours. You must make a reservation. For
UK Eurostar information, tel: 08705-186186; in Brussels, tel: 02-528
2828; <www.eurostar.com>.

Belgian state railways (SNCB/NMBS) operates local services
within Belgium along with international services (tel: 02-528 2828;
<www.b-rail.be> for details).

By Bus. Eurolines operates bus services between all the major
European cities and Brussels (tel: 08705-143219 in the UK, tel: 02-
274 1350 in Belgium for bookings; <www.eurolines.com>).

By Boat. There are car ferry crossings daily to Belgium from the UK (Hull to Zeebrugge) with P&O Ferries (tel: 08705-980333 in the UK; tel: 070-707771 in Belgium; <www.poferries.com>); every two days (Rosyth/Edinburgh to Zeebrugge) with Superfast Ferries (tel: 0870-234 0870 in the UK; tel: 050-252525 in Belgium; <www.superfast.com>) and, for passengers travelling with vehicles only, three times a day (Ramsgate to Ostend) with Transeuropa Ferries (tel: 01843-595522 in the UK; tel: 059-340260 in Belgium; <www.transeuropaferries.com>).

GUIDES AND TOURS (guide/gids)

Brussels has more than 50 guided walking tours (in 14 languages). These are organised by the GBB (Guides of Brussels-Belgium; tel: 02-514 4538), but most programmes do not operate every day. For the Discover Brussels walk, you must pre-arrange an English tour from the Brussels International tourist office.

Calèche or horse-drawn carriage tours of the city centre take place during the summer. Pick them up at rue Charles Buls (Grand-Place) or make a reservation for up to 18 people (tel: 053-700504).

De Boeck's Sightseeing Tours operates bus tours around the city and beyond with multilingual headset accompaniment. You can book these tours through the Brussels International tourist office in the Grand-Place or contact the company directly (tel: 02-633 1580).

H

HEALTH AND MEDICAL CARE

Belgium has a sophisticated health-care system, and many doctors speak English. Medical care is expensive, so ensure that you are insured against illness or accident. For minor treatments, you may have to pay first and reclaim the payment from your insurance company later. Citizens from other European countries can obtain free medical treatment if they carry a European Health Insurance Card.

Most prescription drugs are available in Belgium along with a large range of over-the-counter medications. A pharmacy *(pharmacie/ apotheek)*, indicated by a green cross, will employ a qualified member of staff who will be able to advise you about treatments for minor ailments.

The **Cliniques Universitaires St-Luc**, avenue Hippocrate 10; tel: 02-764 1111, has a casualty/emergency department.

Where's the nearest pharmacy?	**Où est la pharmacie la plus proche?** *Waar is de dichtstbijzijnde apotheek?*
I need a doctor/dentist/ a hospital.	**J'ai besoin d'un médecin/ un dentiste/d'aller a l'hôpital.** *Ik heb een arts/tandarts/ ziekenhuis nodig.*

L

LANGUAGE

About 60 percent of Belgians (mostly in the north of the country) speak Dutch (or *Nederlands*, as the language of Flanders and the Netherlands, is called). In Belgium, you will also hear it described as *Vlaams* – Flemish). In Wallonia (southern Belgium), most of the population speaks French. A small percentage of the population of the eastern part of the country speaks German.

Brussels itself is officially bilingual, with most people speaking French. Menus may be printed in English as well as French and Dutch; if they are not, most staff will be able to explain what things are. You will find that many people in tourist situations speak English. The latter is, in fact, widely spoken, with many English-speaking ex-pats living here. But do try using some French or Dutch, it really will be appreciated. The *Berlitz Phrase Book and Dictionary for French* and *The Berlitz Phrase Book and Dictionary for Dutch* cover most situations you are likely to encounter.

Road signs are in the local language of the region. Many Belgian towns have different names in French and Dutch. For instance, Brussels is *Bruxelles* in French and *Brussel* in Dutch; Bruges is *Brugge* in Dutch; Ghent is *Gent* in Dutch and *Gand* in French; Antwerp is *Antwerpen* in Dutch and *Anvers* in French.

LAUNDRY AND DRY CLEANING

Most hotels will do your laundry for a fee, but it is easy to organise your own laundry and dry cleaning while in town. A centrally located laundromat is Lav O Net, rue Antoine Dansaert 157; tel: 02-219 0562.

MAPS

The Brussels International tourist office produces a comprehensive map and information booklet of central Brussels, ideal for walking tours. The laminated Insight Fleximap is anotther good option.

MEDIA

Newspapers and magazines. English-language newspapers and magazines are available from railway-station kiosks, larger bookshops and newsstands. Expensive hotels often have the *International Herald Tribune, Financial Times* and other quality international newspapers. An English-language weekly news and events magazine, *The Bulletin,* is available in Brussels and other large towns.

Do you have any   **Avez-vous des journaux en anglais?**
English newspapers?   *Hebt u Engelse kranten?*

Radio and television. The BBC World Service and European-based American networks can be picked up easily. Many hotels have cable television with up to 30 channels, including BBC World, Sky News, CNN International and EuroNews.

MONEY

The unit of currency in Belgium is the euro (€), divided into 100 cents. Coins in circulation are €2, €1 and 50, 20, 10, 5, 2 and 1 cents. Banknotes are €500, €200, €100, €50, €20, €10 and €5.

Can I pay by credit card?	**Puis-je payer par carte bancaire?** *Mag ik met mijn kredietkaart betalen?*
I want to change some pounds/dollars.	**Je voudrais changer des livres sterling/dollars.** *Ik wil graag een paar pond/ dollar wisselen.*
Can you cash a travellers cheque?	**Changez-vous les chèques de voyage?** *Kan ik geld voor mijn reis cheque krijgen?*
Where's the nearest bank/ currency exchange office?	**Où est la banque/le bureau de change la/le plus proche?** *Waar is de dichtstbijzijnde bank/ het dichtstbijzijnde wisselkantoor?*
Is there a cash machine here?	**Y a-t-il un distributeur de billets?** *Is er hier ergens een geldautomaat?*
How much is that?	**Combien coûte ceci?** *Hoeveel is dat?*

Exchange facilities. Generally, banks offer the best rates, followed by bureaux de change. Bureaux de change can be found at the airport, at each of Brussels' railway stations and on and around the Grand-Place. Travellers' cheques can be cashed at these locations as long as you have your passport with you. There are currency-exchange machines at Brussels Airport which make transactions in several currencies. Cash machines (ATMs) called 'Bancontact' and 'Mister Cash', which accept non-Belgian cards, are widely available.

Credit cards. Many hotels, restaurants and shops accept payment by international credit cards.

Value-added tax, service charge. A sales (value-added) tax – called TVA in French and BTW in Dutch – is imposed on most goods and services. Hotels, taxi drivers and most restaurants also add a service charge. Both are included in the bill. Some shops operate a tax-refund scheme for non-EU visitors: look for 'Europe Tax-Free Shopping' stickers on the window.

OPENING HOURS

Offices open from 8am or 9am until 5pm or 6pm Mon–Fri.
Banks are open Mon–Fri 9am–4 or 5pm, a few on Sat morning.
Shops are generally open from 10am to 6pm Mon–Sat, but tourist shops may stay open longer and open on Sun. Department stores are generally open until 8pm on Thurs. There are also a number of night-shops in the city selling a range of food, alcohol and other goods until the early hours of the morning. Post offices are open Mon–Fri, 9am–4pm. The post office at Centre Monnaie is open on Sat morning.
Museums are generally open Tues–Sat 10am–5pm, sometimes closing for one hour at lunchtime, usually between 1 and 2pm.

P

POLICE (see also CRIME AND SAFETY and EMERGENCIES)

The police *(police/politie)* can be reached on the emergency **101** telephone number. Officers wear dark-blue uniforms and many of them can speak at least some English. For less urgent police matters, go to **Brussels Central Police Station**, rue du Marché-au-Charbon 30, tel: 02-279 7979, near the Grand-Place.

POST OFFICES (La Poste/De Poste)

Belgian postal services are speedy and reliable. The main post office is at the Centre Monnaie in place de la Monnaie. Belgian post boxes are red with a stylised bugle in relief on the side. Postal rates for postcards and letters up to 50g in weight are 70 or 80 cents within Europe, and 75 or 90 cents for all other destinations.

PUBLIC HOLIDAYS

Belgium's national holiday *(jour férié/openbare feestdag)* days are:

1 January	New Year's Day
1 May	Labour Day
21 July	National Day
15 August	Assumption
1 November	All Saints' Day
11 November	Armistice Day (1918)
25 December	Christmas

Movable dates: Easter Monday, Ascension Day, Pentecost Monday.

PUBLIC TRANSPORT

The Société de Transports Intercommunaux Bruxellois (STIB) runs metro, bus and tram services in the metropolitan area of Brussels. With one ticket you can transfer between trams, metro and buses for a period of one hour (you must re-validate your ticket with each change). Tickets can be purchased from STIB offices, metro stations and newsstands. A ticket for one journey is €1.50 or €2, and a 10-journey ticket costs €11. A one-day pass costs €4. These are available from tourist offices in addition to the other sources above. Maps of the network can be obtained from metro offices and tourist offices. Public transport operates from 6am to midnight.

Metro. Metro/subway/underground stations are indicated by a sign with a white M on a blue background. There are information offices at Gare du Midi, Brouckère, Rogier and Porte de Namur stations.

Trams and buses. An extensive network of trams and buses operates to all parts of the city; trams generally get around faster than buses. Part of the tram network in the city centre operates underground. Red-and-white signs indicate stops for both. Signal the driver to stop if you want to get on. Some tram stops are in the middle of the street, with traffic lanes next to them. Although traffic should stop to allow you to board and alight, take care when getting on and off.

Taxis. Fares start at €2.40 (€4.40 at night), then €1.23 per km (0.6 mile) within greater Brussels. Contact: Taxis Bleus, tel: 02-268 0000; Taxis Oranges, tel: 02-349 4343; or Taxis Verts, tel: 02-349 4949.

Where can I get a taxi?	**Où puis-je trouver un taxi?**
	Waar kan ik een taxi nemen?
What's the fare to...?	**Quel est le prix de la course pour...?**
	Hoeveel kost een rit naar...?
When's the next bus/ train to...?	**A quelle heure est le prochain bus/ train pour...?**
	Wanneer is de volgende bus/ trein naar...?
I want a ticket to...	**Je voudrais un billet pour...**
	Ik wil graag een kaart naar...
single/return	**aller-simple/aller-retour**
	enkele reis/retour
	(also known as **un direct**/*een direkt*)

Trains. Belgian state railways (SNCB/NMBS) operates services to Antwerp, Bruges and Ghent (and many other places). Excursion tickets include the cost of transport and the entrance fee for an attraction in certain areas, and may save you money. Tel: 02-528 2828 for details.

Buses. The bus is not as quick as the train, but for some destinations it is a more convenient option, and in some cases the only one. Walloon Brabant (mostly destinations south of Brussels) services are operated by TEC, tel: 010-235353; Flemish Brabant (mostly destinations north of Brussels) services are operated by De Lijn; tel: 070-220200 for information.

R

RELIGION

Belgium is a predominantly Catholic country, but there are a number of Protestant churches. In Brussels, it is possible to attend English-language services. There are also mosques and synagogues, which hold regular meetings.

T

TELEPHONES

When making international calls, dial 00 followed by the country code: Belgium 32; UK 44; USA and Canada 1; Ireland 353; Australia 61; New Zealand 64; South Africa 27. Most hotels allow direct dialling for international calls, but this can be expensive. Contact an international telephone company to route your call. AT&T, MCI, Sprint, Canada Direct and British Telecom have numbers for this purpose. The call is charged either to your calling card or credit card.

To call another Belgian number inside Belgium, you always need to dial the full area code, even when you are calling a number from within the same area. Some area codes are: Brussels 02, Antwerp 03, Bruges 050, Ghent 09.

Call boxes can be found in all public places in Brussels; those permitting international direct-dial calls show European flags. Machines accept 10 cents, 20 cents, 50 cents, €1 and €2 coins and phone cards *(telecards/telekaarten)*. Phone cards can be purchased in grocery stores, from newsstands, and at post offices and railway stations. Rates for telephone calls are listed in phone kiosks.

TIME ZONES

Belgium is in the Central European Time zone, which is Greenwich Mean Time (GMT), or Universal Coordinated Time (UTC), plus one hour in winter and two hours in summer (between the end of March and the end of October, clocks are advanced one hour). Belgium is one hour ahead of the UK and Ireland, six hours ahead of US Eastern Standard Time (but note that Daylight Saving Time now begins at different times in the US), and 10 hours behind eastern Australia (Sydney).

New York	London	**Belgium**	Jo'burg	Sydney	Auckland
6am	11am	**noon**	1pm	10pm	midnight

TIPPING

Service is included in most bills, so tipping is not necessary. Nevertheless, tips are still appreciated (though not always expected) by some service personnel, particularly in places that cater to a large number of tourists. To tip as Belgians do (when they do at all) in restaurants, round up your bill to the nearest convenient amount or leave about 5 percent. A tip of 10 percent would be considered generous in most cases.

Service is also included in taxi fare rates, so any extra tip is completely at your discretion.

TOILETS

There are public toilets in all metro and railway stations, and in shopping malls (such as Anspach, Centre Monnaie). In many public toilets, 'tipping' the attendant 25–50 cents (or whatever minimum amount is posted) is mandatory. In small cafés and restaurants, men's and women's toilets may be only notionally separated.

Where are the toilets?	**Où sont les toilettes?** *Waar is het WC, alstublieft?*

TOURIST INFORMATION

Brussels has its own tourist information office, which produces maps and information guides to help you on your trip. There is a small charge for some items. It also issues a Brussels Card, valid for 24, 48 or 72 hours, with reductions on the entry prices of numerous attractions and a public transport pass (€20–33). Contact them at:

Brussels International-Tourism Congress, Town Hall (Hôtel de Ville), Grand-Place, 1000 Brussels, tel: 02-513 8940, fax: 02-513 8320, <www.brusselsinternational.be>. There is also an information office at the arrivals lounge of Brussels National Airport, and another in the TGV/Thalys/Eurostar hall at Gare du Midi.

The **Belgian Tourist Office** has international offices:

UK: (Brussels and Wallonia): 217 Marsh Wall, London E14 9FJ, tel: 020-7537 1132, brochure line: 0800-954 5245, fax: 020-7531 0393, <www.belgiumtheplaceto.be>. (Brussels and Flanders): 1a Cavendish Square, London W1G 0LD, tel: 020-7307 7738, brochure line: 0800-954 5245, <www.visitflanders.co.uk>.

US: 220 East 42nd Street, Suite 3402, New York, NY 10017, tel: 212-758 8130, fax: 212-355 7675, <www.visitbelgium.com>.

Canada: English-speaking residents can contact the New York office (*see above*, and by calling tel: 514-457 2888). For French-speaking residents: Office de Promotion de Tourisme Wallonie-Bruxelles,

43 rue de Buade, Bureau 525, Quebec Ville, Quebec G1R 4A2, tel: 418-692 4939, fax: 418-692 4974, <www.visitbelgium.com>.
Brussels: Office de Promotion du Tourisme de Wallonie et de Bruxelles, rue St-Bernard 30, 1060 Brussels, tel: 070-221021, brochure line: 02-509 2400, <www.opt.be>. Toerisme Vlaanderen, rue du Marché-aux-Herbes/Grasmarkt 61–63, 1000 Brussel, tel: 02-504 0390, fax: 02-513 0475, <www.visitflanders.com>.

Where is the tourist office?	**Où est l'office du tourisme?**	*Waar is het verkeers bureau?*

WEBSITES

Here are some websites to help you plan your trip: <www.belgique-tourisme.net>; <www.visitbelgium.com>; <www.belgiumtheplaceto.be>; <www.brusselsinternational.be>; <www.visitflanders.co.uk>; <www.antwerpen.be>; <www.brugge.be>; <www.visitgent.be>.

Y

YOUTH HOSTELS *(auberge de jeunesse/jeugdherberg)*

There are a number of good youth hostels in the city, including three within the central Brussels area (the 1000 postal code area). It is important to make a booking, especially at peak times.
Auberge de Jeunesse Jacques Brel, rue de la Sablonnière 30, tel: 02-218 0187, fax: 02-217 2005, <www.laj.be>. This hostel also has facilities for disabled travellers.
Jeugdherberg Breughel, rue du St-Esprit/Heilige Geeststraat 2, tel: 02-511 0436, fax: 02-512 0711, <www.jeugdherbergen.be>.
Sleep Well, rue du Damier 23, tel: 02-218 5050, fax: 02-218 1313, <www.sleepwell.be>.

Recommended Hotels

Brussels has a large number of hotels ranging from the large and luxurious to the small and simple. Though many hotels rate themselves by the international star system, there is no definitive standard. The national star rating is not necessarily an indication of the style and standard of a hotel, but simply a confirmation that it has certain facilities.

High season comes in the summer months (May–September), with low season in winter (November–March). However, there are rises in demand when large conventions are in town or special events such as the Jazz Marathon take place. Prices are generally lower in winter, though some hotels catering predominantly to business clients offer good discounts for weekend stays throughout the year, as this is when they have spare capacity.

The prices below indicate room rates per night for a double room. Most budget and moderately priced hotels include breakfast in the room rate, but many expensive hotels do not. Older hotels tend not to have wheelchair access, although newer hotels generally have ramps. You should contact an establishment directly if this is a specific requirement. To telephone from abroad, dial your country's international access number, followed by the country code for Belgium (32), followed by one of the numbers listed below (minus the initial 0 of the area code).

€€€€	over 400 euros
€€€	250–400 euros
€€	100–250 euros
€	below 100 euros

BRUSSELS

GRAND-PLACE/ILOT SACRE/FISH MARKET

L'Amigo €€€€ *rue de l'Amigo 1–3, 1000 Brussels; tel: 02-547 4747; fax: 02-513 5277; <www.roccofortehotels.com>.* One of the most elegant hotels in the city, the Amigo is conveniently situated just off the Grand-Place. This luxury hotel makes a relaxing place in which to retreat after a day of sightseeing. Facilities include a restaurant and bar. Breakfast is not included. 174 rooms.

Astrid €€ *place du Samedi 11, 1000 Brussels; tel: 02-219 3119; fax: 02-219 3170; <www.astridhotel.be>*. Modern hotel near St Catherine's Church. Facilities include a restaurant and bar. Breakfast is included. Access for disabled guests. 100 rooms.

Le Dixseptième €€ *rue de la Madeleine 25, 1000 Brussels; tel: 02-517 1717; fax: 02-502 6424; <www.ledixseptieme.be>*. This intimate hotel is just across from the Galeries Royales St-Hubert, so it's very central. The house was home to the Spanish ambassador in the 18th century, and retains much of its grandeur. Today, it's a small hotel offering a different kind of upmarket accommodation, with antique furniture and wood floors. Facilities include a garden and bar. Breakfast is included. 24 rooms.

Floris Grand-Place €€ *rue des Harengs 6–8, 1000 Brussels; tel: 02-514 0760; fax: 02-548 9039; <www.grouptorus.com>*. Many rooms in this small hotel, situated in a historic district and street leading off the Grand-Place, have beams and little windows. They are nicely furnished, but the bathrooms are small. You can't beat the location for both sightseeing and eating out. Breakfast is included. 12 rooms.

Métropole €€€–€€€€ *place de Brouckère 31, 1000 Brussels; tel: 02-217 2300; fax: 02-218 0220; <www.metropolehotel.be>*. The grande-dame of Brussels' hotels, the Métropole is sumptuous, with fantastic marble decorations, although some areas are showing their age. Enjoy a drink at the street terrace café even if you don't book a room – it's the place to be seen. Facilities include a restaurant, bar, fitness room and beauty therapy centre. Breakfast is extra. 305 rooms.

Mozart € *rue du Marché-aux-Fromages 23, 1000 Brussels; tel: 02-502 6661; fax: 02-502 7758; <www.hotel-mozart.be>*. Situated one street behind the Grand-Place in the heart of a restaurant and bar area, the Mozart offers a good budget option to those who want to be very central. Rooms have antique furnishings and old paintings. Breakfast is not included. 50 rooms.

Welcome €–€€ *quai au Bois-à-Brûler 23, 1000 Brussels; tel: 02-219 9546; fax: 02-217 1887; <www.hotelwelcome.com>*. This boutique hotel, in a townhouse dating from 1896 at the Marché-aux-Poissons, makes up in personal attention for what it lacks in size. Each room is individually styled on a different national theme, with antiques and ethnic fittings. There's no shortage of good seafood restaurants just outside on the Fish Market. Breakfast is included. 15 rooms.

UPPER CITY

Astoria Brussels €€€ *rue Royale 103, 1000 Brussels; tel: 02-227 0505; fax: 02-217 1150; <www.sofitel.com>*. This beautiful period hotel has fine public rooms with stained glass and chandeliers. The bedrooms are also in period style, with painted wood panelling. Enjoy the luxury of days gone by, only with the added comfort of modern amenities. Facilities include a restaurant, bar and fitness room. Breakfast is not included. 118 rooms.

Les Bluets € *rue Berckmans 124, 1060 Brussels; tel: 02-534 3983; fax: 02 543 0970; <www.geocities.com/les_bluets>*. In a townhouse dating from 1864 off avenue Louise, this small, quirky – and non-smoking – hotel, filled with antiques, is full of country-house charm. The feeling of staying at a rural residence extends into the rooms, which are old-fashioned and comfortable rather than modern and efficient. Breakfast is included. 6 rooms.

Conrad Brussels €€€€ *avenue Louise 71, 1050 Brussels; tel: 02-542 4242; fax: 02-542 4200; <www.conradhotels.com>*. Large and sprawling, this business-oriented hotel on Brussels' classiest avenue is among the most expensive in town. Facilities include a heated indoor pool, a health club and spa, and a refined French restaurant. There can be few in-room amenities the Conrad has neglected to install in its 269 luxuriously furnished rooms. Breakfast is extra.

De Boeck's €€ *rue Veydt 40, 1050 Brussels; tel: 02-537 4033; fax: 02-534 4037; <www.hotel-deboecks.be>*. In a residential street off busy chaussée de Charleroi, this tranquil hotel is distinguished by graceful décor and antiques in its reception area and hallways. The rooms are plain, however (some of them to a fault), but mostly decently furnished and comfortable. Breakfast is included. 46 rooms.

Hotel du Congrès €€ *rue du Congrès 42, 1000 Brussels; tel: 02-217 1890; fax: 02-217 1897; <www.hotelducongres.be>*. This hotel is just off rue Royale, a few blocks from the Grand-Place. It's a clean, basic option with a generous breakfast included. 70 rooms.

Montgomery €€€€ *avenue de Tervuren 134, 1150 Brussels; tel: 02-741 8511; fax: 02-741 8500; <www.montgomery.be>*. Situated near Parc du Cinquantenaire, the Montgomery offers an English country-house atmosphere in the city. The library has volumes in several languages, and other facilities include a restaurant, bar, comprehensive fitness room and sauna. Breakfast is not included. 63 rooms.

Sabina € *rue du Nord 78, 1000 Brussels; tel: 02-218 2637; fax: 02-219 3239; <www.hotelsabina.be>*. In a street off rue Royale, this small hotel in a 19th-century townhouse features some of the attributes of a private residence. The rooms don't quite match the warmth and homeliness of the public spaces, but are quiet and tastefully modern, and some have kitchenettes. Breakfast is included. 24 rooms.

Warwick Barsey €€€€ *avenue Louise 381–83, 1050 Brussels; tel: 02-649 9800; fax: 02-640 1764; <www.warwickbarsey.com>*. A luxury hotel situated near the historic city centre and only minutes away from the best designer shopping in Brussels (on avenue Louise). The Barsey Mayfair has well-furnished rooms, a bar and friendly helpful staff. Breakfast is not included. 99 rooms.

BEYOND THE OLD CITY

Bedford €€–€€€ *rue du Midi 135–7, 1000 Brussels; tel: 02-507 0000; fax: 02-507 0010; <www.hotelbedford.be>*. The Bedford is close to Gare du Midi. The décor in the rooms is a little unimaginative, and rooms also vary greatly in terms of natural light and noise levels. Restaurant, bar and shops. Breakfast is included. 326 rooms.

Comfort Art Hotel Siru €€ *place Rogier 1, 1210 Brussels; tel: 02-203 3580; fax: 02-203 3303; <www.comforthotelsiru.com>.* Situated on a redeveloped square near Gare du Nord, the Siru is a comfortable hotel with a difference. More than 100 contemporary Belgian artists, including painters, sculptors and comic-strip draughtsmen, have "decorated" the rooms and public areas, so each space makes an individual statement. Facilities include a restaurant and bar. Breakfast is included. 101 rooms.

Le Plaza €€€–€€€€ *boulevard Adolphe Max 118–26, 1000 Brussels; tel: 02-278 0100; fax: 02-278 0101; <www.leplaza-brussels.be>.* Situated just a short stroll from place de Brouckère, Le Plaza was a major attraction for visitors during the 1930s and 1940s, but it passed a number of years in the doldrums before being totally refurbished in fine style in the late 1990s. Unfortunately, its girly-bar neighbours are not quite so salubrious. Le Plaza's facilities include a bar, restaurant, sauna and fitness room. Breakfast is extra. 193 rooms.

Ustel €€ *square de l'Aviation 6–8, 1070 Brussels; tel: 02-520 6053; fax: 02-520 3328; <www.grouptorus.com>.* Friendly three-star hotel just minutes from Gare du Midi. There is a lively bar with a large terrace, and an excellent restaurant sits next door in the old historic flood-lock building of the River Senne. Rooms with kitchenettes are available for longer stays. Breakfast is included. 118 rooms.

ANTWERP

De Witte Lelie €€€ *Keizerstraat 16–18, 2000 Antwerp; tel: 03-226 1966; fax: 03-234 0019; <www.dewittelelie.be>.* Magnificent suites-only hotel just minutes away from the Grote Markt and other attractions in central Antwerp. The courtyard is a peaceful retreat from the bustle of the city. Facilities include a restaurant and bar, and breakfast is included. 10 rooms.

Rubenshof € *Amerikalei 115–17, 2000 Antwerp, tel: 03-237 0789; fax: 03-248 2594; <www.rubenshof.be>.* Near the Royal Museum of Fine Arts, this small family hotel used to be the residence of

Belgium's cardinal and features lavishly appointed public spaces. The rooms are plain, but comfortable. 22 rooms.

BRUGES

Hans Memling €–€€ *Kuiperstraat 18, 8000 Bruges; tel: 050-471212; fax: 050-471210; <www.grouptorus.com>*. A small hotel situated in the heart of the city, the Hans Memling is perfect for exploring this historic town. Pleasant breakfast room (breakfast is included). There is a bar. 36 rooms.

De Orangerie €€€ *Karthuizerinnenstraat 10, 8000 Bruges; tel: 050-341649; fax: 050-333016; <www.hotelorangerie.com>*. An attractive 17th-century canal house set opposite the Dijver canal, this hotel is in an ideal location. The rooms are individually designed and furnished to luxurious standards. There is a bar, and guests have the use of the sauna and pool of the Tuilerieen Hotel (a sister hotel) on the opposite side of the road. Breakfast is included. 20 rooms.

Rosenburg €€ *Coupure 30, 8000 Bruges; tel: 050-340194; fax: 050-345539; <www.rosenburg.be>*. A 10-minute walk from the historic centre, this quiet, canalside hotel offers modern yet comfortable accommodation. There is a restaurant and bar, and breakfast is included. 22 rooms.

GHENT

Novotel Gent Centrum €€€ *Goudenleeuwplein 5, 9000 Ghent; tel: 09-224 2230; fax: 09-224 3295; <www.novotel.com>*. Part of the Novotel chain, this is probably one of its most attractive hotels. Situated in the centre of Ghent, it incorporates a 14th-century crypt. Restaurant, bar and pool. Breakfast is not included. 117 rooms.

Sofitel Gent Belfort €€€€ *Hoogpoort 63, 9000 Ghent; tel: 09-233 3331; fax: 09-233 1102; <www.sofitel.com>*. Situated opposite the Stadhuis (Town Hall), the Sofitel is centrally located and in a perfect position for exploring the town. Facilities include a restaurant, bar, fitness room and sauna. Breakfast is extra. 174 rooms.

Recommended Restaurants

In most of the finer restaurants listed below, it is best to make a reservation; for a few of them, you will need to book weeks in advance or hope for a last-minute cancellation.

Keep in mind that many restaurants accept dogs in the dining room and on outside terraces. Smoking is no longer permitted in restaurants in Belgium, but it is allowed in bars, cafés and snackbars. The following prices are for dinner for one person without wine. If you want to make a reservation from outside Belgium, dial your country's international access number, followed by the country code for Belgium (32) and one of the numbers listed below (minus the initial 0 of the area code).

€€€€	over 100 euros
€€€	60–100 euros
€€	30–60 euros
€	below 30 euros

BRUSSELS

GRAND-PLACE/ILOT SACRE/FISH MARKET

La Belle Maraîchère €€ *place Ste-Catherine 11a; tel: 02-512 9759.* Seafood delivered fresh from the coast is the speciality at this restaurant. It is served in a range of dishes. The fishermen's stew is highly regarded. Open Fri–Tues, lunch noon–2.30pm, dinner 6–10pm.

Chez Léon € *rue des Bouchers 18; tel: 02-511 1415.* Mussels are big in Belgium, and nowhere more so than at this mussels specialist near the Grand-Place – something that has been the case since 1893. It's not fancy, and the approach even verges on fast-food, but there's nothing wrong with its mollusc speciality, served in a variety of ways, the most basic of which is *marinières* (steamed in a vegetable stock). Open Sun–Thur, 11.30am–11pm, Fri–Sat 11.30am–11.30pm.

Comme Chez Soi €€€€ *place Rouppe 22; tel: 02-512 2921.* Pierre Wynants, the proprietor of this restaurant, which has three

Michelin stars, is one of the world's most creative chefs. The restaurant is styled in early-20th-century Art Nouveau style in homage to Victor Horta. The dishes use the best of local ingredients – a delight for the senses. You can eat in the dining room or take one of the tables in the kitchen. Book as early as possible or try for a last-minute cancellation. Jacket and tie required. Open Tues–Sat lunch noon–2pm, dinner 7–10pm. Closed national holidays and all of July.

L'Ecailler du Palais Royal €€€ *rue Bodenbroeck 18; tel: 02-512 8751.* This restaurant offers a gastronomic event featuring exquisite seafood, fine wine and impeccable service. The *plat du jour* is a great budget option at lunchtime. Open lunch noon–2.30pm, dinner 7–10.30pm. Closed Sun, national holidays and Aug.

In 't Spinnekopke €€ *place du Jardin-aux-Fleurs 1; tel: 02-511 8695.* Said to be the oldest tavern in Brussels, In 't Spinnekopke serves ample portions of Flemish dishes, which are accompanied by a choice of more than 100 Belgian beers. You'll find it just beyond place St-Géry. Open Mon–Fri, lunch noon–3pm, dinner 6–11pm; Sat dinner only.

't Kelderke €–€€ *Grand-Place 15; tel: 02-513 7344.* A typical Brussels bar/restaurant hidden away in a cellar room below the Grand-Place. It serve the very best Flemish dishes, all washed down with excellent beer. The place has an informal atmosphere and is always noisy and very busy because it's such good value. Open daily noon–2am.

La Maison du Cygne €€€€ *rue Charles Buls 2; tel: 02-511 8244.* Originally home of the butcher's guild before becoming a tavern frequented by Marx and Engels, this place is now one of the best restaurants in town, specialising in French dishes. In addition to the delicious food, the ornate dining room on the second floor has great views over the Grand-Place. Open Mon–Fri, lunch 11am–3pm, dinner 7.15–10pm; Sat dinner only. Closed during Aug.

La Manufacture €€ *rue Notre-Dame du Sommeil 12–20; tel: 02-502 2525.* A beacon of good taste in a former designer leather-goods factory, in an unprepossessing neighbourhood. You dine on French-based world cuisine, amid iron pillars and exposed air ducts in the refurbished workshop; for the décor, think wood floors, leather benches, polished wood and stone tables. On sunny summer days, the shaded outdoor terrace is a pleasant place on which to eat. Open Mon–Fri noon–2pm and 7–11pm, Sat 7pm–midnight.

De l'Ogenblik €€ *galerie des Princes 1; tel: 02-511 6151.* On the edge of the Galeries Royales St-Hubert, this restaurant combines the simple décor of a chic French brasserie with Belgian service and a Franco-Belgian menu of meat and seafood dishes. Open Mon–Sat, lunch noon–2.30pm, dinner 7pm–midnight.

La Roue d'Or €€ *rue des Chapeliers 26; tel: 02-514 2554.* This Art Deco brasserie has murals inspired by Magritte. If you can manage to keep your appetite in the profusion of silver gilt, you will enjoy a typical Belgian menu, which also has a few French dishes. Open daily noon–12.30am.

LE SABLON/LES MAROLLES

Bleu de Toi €€€ *rue des Alexiens 73; tel: 02-502 4371.* Pretty restaurant on a street just west of the church of Notre Dame de la Chapelle. There are three small intimate dining areas, including a vine-covered terrace. The menu is based on French cuisine with modern twists. Open lunch noon–2pm, dinner 7.30–11.30pm, closed Sat lunch and all day Sun.

La Canne à Sucre €€ *rue des Pigeons 12; tel: 02-513 0372.* Come here for cuisine from the French Antilles–Martinique. Boudin sausage, *court bouillon* piquant sauces and conch stew are all specialities worth trying. You will also find splendid Martinique rum. Open Tues–Sat, dinner only 7.30pm–midnight. Closed during the week of 21 July.

La Grande Porte €€–€€€ *rue Notre Seigneur 9; tel: 02-512 8998.* Very informal eatery with friendly staff. The traditional Belgian dishes come in enormous portions, so bring your appetite. Good range of beers and reasonable house wine. Open lunch noon–3pm, dinner 6pm–2am. Closed Sat lunch and all day Sun.

Au Stekerlapatte €€ *rue des Prêtres 4; tel: 02-512 8681*. Brussels roast chicken and pig's feet are two of the specialities in this brasserie behind the Palais du Justice. A local favourite. Open Wed–Sun, dinner 7pm–1am.

BEYOND THE OLD CITY

Bruneau €€€€ *avenue Broustin 73–5; tel: 02-421 7070*. Occupying a nicely decorated town house a little way from the centre, near the National Basilica of the Sacred Heart, the long-established Bruneau is one of the best restaurants in Brussels and has a faithful following. Contemporary and imaginative gastronomic menu; outdoor dining in summer. Open Thur–Mon, lunch noon–2.30pm, dinner 7–10pm.

Le Chalet de la Forêt €€€ *drève de Lorraine 43; tel: 02-374 5416*. Fine French cuisine is served in the elegant dining room or on the terrace. Le Chalet is situated at the edge of the Forêt de Soignes, making it a perfect lunch venue on your excurions to the Waterloo battlefield or Tervuren. Open Mon–Fri, lunch noon–2.30pm, dinner 7–10.30pm.

La Grand Ecluse €€–€€€ *boulevard Poincaré 77; tel: 02-522 3025*. Just across the *petite ceinture*, this restaurant was once a lock house for the river and canal system, and the beautifully renovated lock mechanism adds to the innovative overall design. There is a terrace at the rear. The excellent food is based on French cuisine. Open Sun–Wed lunch noon–2.30pm, Thur–Sat noon–2.30pm and dinner 7–11pm.

UPPER CITY

La Quincaillerie €€–€€€ *rue du Page 45; tel 02-533 9833*. Situated near the Musée Horta, this restaurant is housed in a late-

19th-century warehouse. The industrial feel has been kept in the truly splendid décor, and the whole place hums with chatter. A typical brasserie with a twist. Belgian and continental dishes are on the menu here. Open lunch Mon–Fri noon–2.30pm, dinner daily 7pm–midnight.

De Ultieme Hallucinatie €€–€€€ *rue Royale 316; tel: 02-217 0614*. Near Le Botanique, this brasserie is famed for its Art Nouveau interior, created in 1904. There is a restaurant with a French haute cuisine menu for formal service, and a brasserie for quick, less formal service. Restaurant open Mon–Fri lunch noon–2.30pm, dinner 7–10.30pm; Sat dinner only. Brasserie open Mon–Fri 11am–2.30am, Sat and Sun 3pm–2am.

Au Vieux Bruxelles €€ *rue St-Boniface 35; tel: 02-503 3111*. Situated close to the Porte Namur, this traditional restaurant is a proud purveyor of that Belgian seafood obsession, *moules*, served in a multiplicity of styles. It's been in business since 1882 and its mussels show no sign of flagging. Open Tues–Thur 6.30–11.30pm, Fri–Sat 6.30pm–midnight, Sun noon–3pm and 6.30–11.30pm.

ANTWERP

Rooden Hoed €€ *Oude Koornmarkt 25, tel: 03-233 2844*. Reputed to be Antwerp's oldest restaurant, this establishment, situated near the cathedral, is 250 years old. Rooden Hoed provides hearty quantities of regional Belgian and French dishes, some of them old standbys and some modern. Open daily noon–2.30pm and 6–10.30pm.

Sir Anthony Van Dijck €€–€€€ *Oude Koornmarkt 16 (Vlaeykensgang), tel: 03-231 6170*. Occupying a superb location in the restored 16th-century Vlaeykensgang courtyard, this modern French-Flemish restaurant is a labour of love for its owner/chef, who removed himself from Michelin-star stress to do something that was considerably more to his liking. The result is a relaxed experience and memorable cuisine. Open Mon–Sat noon–2pm and 6.30–10pm.